Translating Ningbo

Editors   Anfang HE   Xia XIANG

Dawn on Civilization
Prehistory of Ningbo

东方曙光　宁波史前文明

Author

Weijin HUANG

Translators

Yanfei WU

Zhanfeng FANG

Reviewer

Tiezhu DONG

ZHEJIANG UNIVERSITY PRESS
浙江大学出版社
·杭州·

宁波出版社
NINGBO PUBLISHING HOUSE

图书在版编目（CIP）数据

东方曙光：宁波史前文明 = Dawn on Civilization:
Prehistory of Ningbo：英文 / 黄渭金著；吴燕飞，房战峰译
. -- 杭州：浙江大学出版社，2022.12（2023.10重印）
（宁波文化译丛 / 贺安芳，项霞总主编）
ISBN 978-7-308-23241-8

Ⅰ.①东… Ⅱ.①黄… ②吴… ③房… Ⅲ.①史前文
化－文化史－宁波－英文 Ⅳ.①K295.53

中国版本图书馆CIP数据核字（2022）第212677号

东方曙光：宁波史前文明
Dawn on Civilization: Prehistory of Ningbo

黄渭金　著　　　吴燕飞　房战峰　译　　　董铁柱　译审

策划编辑　黄静芬
责任编辑　黄静芬
责任校对　田　慧
封面设计　周　灵
出版发行　浙江大学出版社
　　　　　（杭州天目山路148号　邮政编码：310007）
　　　　　（网址：http://www.zjupress.com）
排　　版　浙江大千时代文化传媒有限公司
印　　刷　浙江新华数码印务有限公司
开　　本　710mm×1000mm　1/16
印　　张　13
印　　张　8
字　　数　248千
版 印 次　2022年12月第1版　2023年10月第2次印刷
书　　号　ISBN 978-7-308-23241-8
定　　价　60.00元

浙江大学出版社市场运营中心联系方式：　（0571）88925591；http://zjdxcbs.tmall.com

The Unearthed Seeds

The Restored Stilt Style Architecture

A Tenon with a Pin Hole

A Wooden Component with Mortises on Both Ends

The Bone Scyth

The Stone Knife

Well Preserved Grains of Rice

The Pottery Lamb

Pottery Pellets

The Gorgon Fruit

The Poterry *Gui*

The Pottery *Ding*

The Pottery *Dou*

The Pottery *He*

The Pottery *Yu*

The Pottery *Zeng*

The Well at the Tianluoshan Site

Oars of Different Shapes Excavated at the Hemudu Site

The Wooden Weft Beater

The Pottery Spindle Whorl

The Rope on the Ear of a Jar Excavated at the Hemudu Site

The Pottery *He* with a Bright Red Coating

The Cord Pattern on the Pottery *Fu*

The Wooden Shovel

The Jade *Jue*

The Decorative Piece Made of Fish Bone

The Pottery Fish

The Symmetrical Bird-shaped Wooden Artifact

The Bird-shaped Ivory Artifact Decorated with the Sun-pattern

The Bird-shaped Wooden Artifact Painted in Black Laquer

The Double-bird Wooden Artifact

The Eagle-shaped Pottery *Dou*

总　序

宁波历史悠久，文化璀璨；宁波历史文化研究著述丰富，成绩斐然。然而，如何让宁波文化走出国门，如何向世界讲好宁波故事，却一直是个薄弱环节。这与宁波自古以来就崇尚开放的城市禀性不够合拍，也与今天"滨海宁波，扬帆世界"的时代追求不相协调。

有鉴于此，宁波大学科学技术学院人文学院翻译专业教师团队大胆提出：将宁波出版社 2014 年精心推出的"宁波文化丛书"（第一辑）翻译成英文版，让这套丛书作为文化使者，把宁波历史、宁波文明、宁波精神、宁波智慧带到四面八方。

"宁波文化丛书"（第一辑）共 8 本，出于一些原因，我们替换了其中 1 本，因此这套"宁波文化译丛"也是 8 本。具体是：王耀成著《商行四海：解读宁波帮》，黄定福著《奇构巧筑：宁波建筑文化》，谢安良著《丝路听潮：海上丝绸之路文化》，黄渭金著《东方曙光：宁波史前文明》，涂师平著《羽人竞渡：宁波发展史话》，方同义著《千年文脉：浙东学术文化》，虞浩旭、张爱妮著《甬藏书香：宁波藏书文化》，郁伟年著《阿拉宁波人》。

得益于原作者在挖掘、整理和研究宁波历史文化方面所做出的艰苦努力，文质兼美的文本为我们的翻译工作奠定了良好的基础。

但是，要忠实地翻译原著并不是一件容易的事情。以古文翻译为例，上述著作都或多或少征引了古代文献，有的不仅数量很多，而且专业性很强。对于古代文献，中文著作往往直接引用原文，至于古文如何解读可以让读者自己去琢磨。译著则不同，必须做到字字落实，不能含糊，所以翻译起来特别费时费力。我们还经常碰到引用的古文有文字错讹的情况，那就更加考验译者的学问和识见了。一边做翻译，一边查资料，一本书翻译下来，硬是把英语老师磨炼成古文通了。

这只是翻译三要素"信、达、雅"中"信"的问题。而译者追求的不仅仅是"信"，还有"达"与"雅"。翻译不是简单的语言转换，其实是一种再创造。为了向读者奉献一套质量上乘的译丛，我们采取译者精心打磨、同事互相切磋、专家审读把关等措施，把精品意识贯穿于翻译工作的全过程。我们希望我们的译作对得起优秀的宁波文化，也对得起自己的职业操守。

在译丛即将面世之际，我们衷心感谢原作者的创造性劳动，感谢浙江大学出版社和宁波出版社的大力支持，感谢审稿专家和责任编辑的辛勤付出，感谢贺安芳、项霞两位总主编的精心组织和策划。

限于时间和水平，这套译丛也可能存在这样那样的不足甚至错误，欢迎专家和读者提出批评意见。

本译丛是我院翻译团队在译介宁波文化方面迈出的第一步。万事开头难，有了第一步就可以有第二步、第三步……我们将继续努力，为传播宁波历史文化做出自己应有的贡献。

周志锋

2022 年 11 月 11 日

于宁波大学科学技术学院

CONTENTS

001   **Part 1**   **A Sketch of Ningbo's Historic Cultures**

006   Ⅰ. The Hemudu Culture

042   Ⅱ. The Liangzhu Culture

048   Ⅲ. Archeology of the Shang and Zhou Dynasties

057   **Part 2**   **The Dawn in the East**

059   Ⅰ. Environmental Changes

064   Ⅱ. A Marvel in the History of Architecture

074   Ⅲ. A Milestone in Rice Farming

084   Ⅳ. Domestication of Dogs and Pigs

090   Ⅴ. Gathering, Fishing and Hunting

099   Ⅵ. Rice as the Staple Food and Fish as the Main Dish

106   Ⅶ. Wells

112   Ⅷ. Pioneers of Marine Culture

116   Ⅸ. Knitting and Weaving

123   Ⅹ. Handicrafts

134   Ⅺ. Aesthetics

144   Ⅻ. Sun God's Hometown

152   ⅩⅢ. The Origins and Evolution of the Hemudu Culture

162   ⅩⅣ. The Integration into the Liangzhu Culture

169   ⅩⅤ. The Ancestors of the Baiyue People

179   Glossary

200   译后记

Part 1

A Sketch of Ningbo's Historic Cultures

It is generally agreed that Ningbo has a history dating back to at least 7,000 years ago. This conclusion is based on the discovery and study of the Hemudu culture (河姆渡文化) in the early 1970s, which provides valuable reference for the investigation into the early prehistoric society of Ningbo.

Ningbo is an important port city on the southeast coast of China and the economic center of the south flank of the Yangtze River Delta. It is located in the middle of China's continental coastline, on the shore of the East China Sea. It has Zhoushan Islands as a natural barrier against the ocean to its east, and faces Shanghai across Hangzhou Bay to its north. It borders Shaoxing on its west, and adjoins Taizhou on its south, forming Sanmen Bay (三门湾) in the angle.

Ningbo covers a total area of 9,816 square kilometers[1]. The terrain slopes downward from the southwest to the northeast. The Tiantai Mountains (天台山) extend into Ningbo from the southwest, wind across Ninghai County and Xiangshan County to the northeast roughly along the Fenghua River (奉化江) and the Yongjiang River (甬江), and finally pull into the sea, forming the coastal islands. The Siming Mountains (四明山), a branch of the Tiantai Mountains, also known as the Gouyu[2] Mountains (句余山), extend to Yuyao County from the northwest and run along the Fenghua River and the Yongjiang River. According to the book *A Record of the Siming Mountains* (《四明山志》), "The Siming Mountains cover an area of about eight hundred square *li*. Two hundred and eighty peaks stand high next to each other. The five peaks in the middle form the shape of a lotus flower or

---

① 行政区划和区划面积 [EB/OL]. [2022-01-10]. http://www.ningbo.gov.cn/col/col122910 1992/index.html.

② Gouyu (句余) means the end of Gouzhang City (句章城) , the ancient city of Ningbo.

a star. On the peak with a flat top, there is a stone cave with four window-like holes on the rock, letting in the light of the sun, the moon, and stars. So came the name Siming[①] " Two big rivers, the Yuyao River (余姚江) and the Fenghua River, originate from the Siming Mountains, and converge into the Yongjiang River at Sanjiangkou[②] (三江口) in the downtown area. And then the two rivers flow northeast into the East China Sea, passing the Zhaobao Hill (招宝山). The alluvial plain of these rivers near the coast has been regarded as the "land of fish and rice" for its fertile land, rich natural resources, and criss-cross waterways.

Located in the subtropical monsoon climate zone, Ningbo has a warm climate with four distinct seasons and abundant rainfall. The annual average temperature is 16.4℃ . The highest monthly temperature is 28.0℃ , in July, and the lowest is 5.4 ℃ , in January. The city has a frost-free period of 230 to 240 days and a crop growing season of 300 days on average. The annual average precipitation is about 1,480 millimeters, but about 60% of which occurs from May to September during the plum rain season and the typhoon season.[③]

As a historical and cultural city at the national level (国家级历史文化名城), Ningbo has 1,080 cultural relics under protection.[④] They are classified into ten series according to their themes, namely prehistoric cultural sites (史前文化系列), ancient libraries (藏书文化系列), historic sites of overseas transportation (海外交通史系列), historic sites of sea defense (海防史迹系列), historic sites of Eastern Zhejiang School (浙东学派史迹系列), ancient and memorial architectures (古建筑与纪念建筑系列), ruins of Yue celadon kiln (越窑青瓷窑地系列), ancient irrigation sites, revolutionary sites, and other important sites in relation with modern history (近代史迹

---

①   In Chinese, "*si*" means four, and "*ming*" means light.
②   In Chinese, "*san*" means three, "*jiang*" means river, and "*kou*" means mouth. The name "Sanjiangkou" means the spot where three rivers merge.
③   宁波气候 [EB/OL]. [2022-05-11]. http://www.qx121.com/weather/weatherStatic/climateSurvey/index.html.
④   文物保护总介 [EB/OL]. [2022-01-14]. http://www.nbwb.net/pd_wwbh/newslist.aspx?NodeCode=00030001.

系列).

The term "prehistory", first used by the British scholar Daniel Wilson (丹尼尔·威尔逊) in *The Archaeology and Prehistoric Annals of Scotland* (《 苏格兰考古与史前学年鉴 》, 1851), generally refers to human history before the emergence of written records. The timeline of human prehistory is very long and covers the Paleolithic, the Mesolithic, and the Neolithic Periods. People tend to regard prehistory as the childhood of the human race. With no written records, only a limited number of prehistoric legends have been passed down, but their contents are fragmented, sometimes having been reinvented or even made up by later generations. Therefore, to uncover the truth of prehistory, only the archeological evidence is reliable. Prehistory ended at different times across the world, for the time of the emergence of writing systems varies around the world. Generally speaking, the prehistoric period in China began about 1.7 million years ago with the activity of Yuanmouensis (元谋人) in Yunnan as a symbol, and ended in the 21st century BC with the establishment of the Xia Dynasty as a symbol.[1] However, due to China's vast territory, there were great differences in the development of productivity and civilization in different regions. Since most Chinese history literature focuses on the Yellow River Region, Ningbo, far away from the ancient political and cultural center of the central plains (中原地区) in China, turned up in written records very late. Therefore, Ningbo remained in the prehistoric period when dynasties like Shang and Zhou had already governed the central plains. For its remoteness and the lack of written records, Ningbo was then regarded as "a barbarian land" by people from the central plains. However, archeological findings show that actually it was not the case. In fact, the industrious and wise ancients created brilliant prehistoric cultures in Ningbo, with the Hemudu culture as a typical example.

---

[1]　Disputes over the beginning of Chinese history is not yet settled, since no written document in the Xia Dynasty has been found. But the archeological cricle in China used to regard the Xia Dynasty as the starting of history.

I. The Hemudu Culture

Regional archeology in Ningbo began in the 1930s, when the first official institution of cultural relics, the Ningbo Museum of Antiquities (宁波古物陈列所), was established. But archeology in the modern sense did not start until the founding of the People's Republic of China. In the 1950s and 1960s, the archeological work in Ningbo mainly focused on the excavation of ancient tombs and kilns. It was not until the 1970s that a major breakthrough was made. In the summer of 1973, an accidental discovery in Hemudu Village (河姆渡村) of Yuyao County[①] marked the prelude to the study of Ningbo's prehistoric culture, dating back to around 7,000 years ago, and shocked the archeological and historical circles. From then on, the prehistoric culture of Ningbo gained a resounding name, "the Hemudu culture". Hemudu, the representative of the birthplaces of ancient cultures in the Yangtze River Region, has since been written into history textbooks.

Like many other great findings in the world, the Hemudu Site (河姆渡遗址) was discovered by accident. Hemudu Village belonged to a low-lying commune named Luojiang (罗江). The Yuyao River used to flood frequently, especially in the plum rain season and the typhoon season. Therefore, leaders at all levels attached great importance to the maintenance of irrigation facilities, which played an important role in agriculture. In June 1973, to improve the drainage capacity of the old drainage station by the Yuyao River, the officials of the commune decided to extend the station. The station was located on the west of the area now assigned as the Hemudu Site. It was when digging the foundation that the local farmers discovered the Hemudu Site. At a depth of 3 meters, the farmers came across the cultural layer (文

---

① 历史人文 [EB/OL]. [2022-01-15]. http://www.yy.gov.cn/col/col1229133521/.

化层) of the site. But they did not know anything about archeology and went on digging. Thus, a lot of pottery pieces, bone artifacts, animal bones, and a few stone tools were turned over together with the soil. At this critical moment, Luo Chunhua (罗春华), the deputy director of Luojiang Commune (罗江公社), came to check the construction progress. The farmers complained that the digging was very difficult because the soil was always mixed with stones, tiles (板瓦), bones, and wood. Luo felt that the place was likely to have been an important ancient site, and immediately had the objects collected from the farmers' houses for safekeeping. He then phoned the cultural center of Yuyao County. Hearing this news, the cultural center immediately sent a group led by Xu Jinyao (许金耀) to inspect the construction site. Mr. Xu estimated that this should be a site with abundant relics and a long history. He reported it to the officials, and asked them to inform the Administrative Committee of Cultural Relics of Zhejiang Province (浙江文物管理委员会).

After that, he phoned the local administrative officials, and asked for the suspension of the construction and preservation of the scene. The construction was shut down for three days. And the Administrative Committee of Cultural Relics of Zhejiang Province designated Wang Shilun[1] (王士伦) to inspect the site, who was working on the nearby Baoguo Temple (保国寺). On arrival, Mr. Wang was immediately shocked at the abundant relics. He believed it was a Neolithic site which was discovered for the first time of the same kind in Zhejiang Province. So he took some of the objects to Hangzhou, the capital of Zhejiang Province, and reported this to his superiors. Three days later, a group of archeologists led by Wang Jiying[2] (汪济英) started the rescue excavation at Hemudu. A world-famous cultural site was thus discovered under such an unexpected circumstance.

---

[1] Wang Shilun (1929–1998) was a famous scholar on archeology, and worked on the excavation and protection of many cultural relics in Zhejiang Province.

[2] Wang Jiying (1928–2018) was a famous scholar on archeology, and a famous calligrapher.

We owe great thanks to Luo Chunhua. Had it not been for his consciousness of cultural conservation and the seriousness with which he took the site, we would have missed the opportunity to make such a world-famous archeological discovery. In fact, people had missed many such chances before, particularly in the 1960s, when an 80-meter-long irrigation ditch was dug right through the center of the site. As the local people had too little archeological knowledge of the existence of the relic site, the cultural reservation departments were unlikely to get relevant information from them. Even worse, some relics, particularly fine woodwork dug out of the site, were burned for cooking, as no one was aware of their cultural values. Athough only a native-born cadre, Luo Chunhua was an exception, for he had once attended a short-term course on geology in Zhejiang Agicultural University (浙江农业大学) in 1959. And in 1962, when a group from Zhejiang Agricultural University came to Luojiang for soil investigation, he was told by a teacher that a long time before, the local area had been submerged in the sea, and that it emerged as land only recently. Therefore, when so many things were unearthed, he thought the findings might be a sinking ship and paid much attention to the site, for he remembered that timbers and piles were often dug out in the past by farmers working on ditch-digging. Never had he expected it to be such an important Neolithic site.

Three trial pits were dug, one at the construction site of the drainage station, one in the northeast, and one in the south. Two cultural layers were distinguished. It is very important to distinguish cultural layers. It is also the most difficult and basic work in the excavation of an ancient cultural site. If the relics of different cultural layers are mixed, it is impossible to investigate the history of the site, and further research would lack a scientific basis. The archeological term — "cultural layer" is borrowed from the concept of stratum in geology. But it is different from the geological sense, mostly in that it involves human activities in the formation process. Geological strata are formed by natural forces, such as transportation and deposition by wind and running water. Archeological "cultural layers" refer to the strata formed by human activities, such as the excavating, plowing, backfilling or other processing of soil, the disposing of daily life garbage, building rubble or other wastes. One of the most basic principles in archeology is that if an ancient cultural site has more than two cultural layers, one superimposed on another, and they have never been influenced by any external force, the upper layer is the later one. According to this principle, we can judge the relative age of the cultural layers. During the trial excavation, the Hemudu Site cultural deposits were divided into two cultural layers: red pottery pieces were unearthed from the upper layer, black pottery pieces from the lower layer. This was completely contrary to the discovery that red pottery pieces tended to be unearthed from the earlier (lower) cultural layer and black pieces from the later (upper) layer in areas like Hangzhou, Jiaxing, and Huzhou in Zhejiang Province. Besides, a large number of pottery pieces unseen before were unearthed, proving the necessity for more serious archeological work. Thus, in the later half of 1973, the decision to carry out the first scientific excavation was made.

From November 4, 1973 to January 10, 1974, the first excavation was carried out in the grain-drying field in the north of Dutou Village (渡头村). A total of 6 trial trenches and 28 trial pits were dug, covering an area of 800 square meters. The actual excavation area was 630 square meters, as no cultural layers were found in several grids near the Yuyao River as a result of its fluviraption. When they tried to further divide the two cultural layers into four, the ruins of stilt houses and wells were discovered, and more than 1,600 intact pieces of relics with regional characteristics were unearthed, including black charcoal-tempered pottery and bone *si* (耜，plow), otherwise known as bone spades or bone shovels (锨). Also unearthed were a large number of animal and plant remains. An abundance of cultivated rice and many houses built on wooden stilts were excavated, which had never been seen in other sites of the same period. All these significant discoveries immediately caused a great sensation at home and abroad and drew much attention from the academic community.

In 1974, as the experts in Zhejiang Province could not reach a decisive conclusion on these newly discovered things, they sent some of the relics to Beijing. However, there were as many disputes among the experts in Beijing. Thus, in April 1976, "Symposium on the First Phase of Hemudu Archeological Excavation"（河姆渡遗址第 1 次考古发掘座谈会 ）was held in Hangzhou, where the experts and scholars came to an agreement that the 3rd and 4th layers of the Hemudu Site should be named "the Hemudu culture", the 2nd layer is an equivalent to the Majiabang culture（马家浜文化), and the 1st layer is an equivalent to the Songze culture（崧泽文化). The consensus was accepted by the archeological community in China. This was accepted by the archeological community in China. In 1978, "Excavations (First Season) at Ho-Mu-Tu in Yu-Yao County, Chekiang Province"（《 河姆渡遗址第一期发掘报告 》) was published in the first issue of *Journal of Archeology* (《考古学报》).

The first excavation was fruitful, and a preliminary understanding of the cultural value of the Hemudu Site was gained. However, due to the limited area of excavation, many questions were unanswered, and there wasn't enough literature which could explain the relics and remains. To get a clearer picture of the Hemudu Site, experts and scholars from all over the country at the 1976 symposium called for a large-scale excavation. Thus, Zhejiang Revolutionary Committee issued a specific document by the code "Zhejiang Revolution (77) 27", requiring that "the cultural features of the Hemudu Site be clarified in the next few years". Accordingly, the departments of cultural relics and archeology in Zhejiang Province began the preparations for the second excavation of the Hemudu Site.

From October 8, 1977 to January 28, 1978, a second excavation was carried out in a paddy field 20 meters north of the site of the first excavation, covering an area of 2,000 square meters. This excavation verified the previous division of cultural layers, and subdivided the 2nd and 3rd cultural layers into three sub-layers A, B, and C, and the 4th cultural layer into two sub-layers A and B. A total of 4,700 intact pieces of relics were found, including objects made of earth materials, wood, stone, and bone. Twenty-seven tombs and twenty-eight ash pits were found scattered around the area. From the ruins of a vast stretch of wooden stilt houses, the experts figured out the evolution of dwellings from the early houses rested on stilts half driven into the ground (打桩立桩), to the later houses built on layers of sintered soil blocks and pottery fragments on the ground. A large area of rice accumulation, a large number of animal and plant remains, objects of woven reeds and ropes, and a total of more than 200,000 pottery pieces were excavated, among which more than 50,000 pottery pieces were numbered and many wood piles were buried again for preservation after being registered and sketched. A leading group of excavation was set up in Ningbo, and many people participated in this excavation, including members from the Administrative Committee of Cultural Relics of Zhejiang Province, Zhejiang Provincial Museum (浙江省博物馆), and Zhejiang Museum of Natural History (浙江自然博物馆), and some outstanding overseas professionals. "The First Archeological Training Class for Half-farmers-half-workers"[1] (浙江省第一届亦工亦农考古培训班) was hosted. After more than three months of training, the participants returned as the backbones of local archeological work. A group of famous academics arrived and were engaged in this excavation. Su Bingqi (苏秉琦), a nationally famous archeologist, and Yan Wenming (严文明), a professor from Peking University, guided the excavation in person; Yang Hongxun (杨鸿勋), an expert in ancient architecture and Liu Zechun (刘泽纯), a professor of geology at Nanjing University, analyzed the ruins of wood buildings and the geological features of the site.

The second excavation provided a number of new materials for the

---

[1] "Half-farmer-half-workers" were a group of people, who were engaged in industrial production or local administrative work, but had their registered permanent residence in the rural areas. They were distinguished from workers who had registered permanent residence in the urban areas. It was a peculiar phenomenon caused by the household registration system in China.

rediscovery of the cultural features of the Hemudu Site and the inner connection among the four cultural layers, proving that the four cultural layers were closely related to each other, all belonging to the Hemudu culture. The report titled "The Second Excavation of the Hemudu Site in Zhejiang Province" (《 浙江河姆渡遗址第二次发掘的主要收获 》) was published in the fifth issue of *Cultural Relics* in 1980.

In archeology, the term "culture", just like "cultural layer", also has its specific meaning. In modern times, the word "culture" generally refers to the superstructure and all aspects of spiritual life, for example, the human achievements in science, technology, art, and education. Archeologically, "culture" refers to the material culture, such as various production tools, utensils, artworks, and ornaments created by human beings. As far as the naming of a culture is concerned, two things are worth mentioning. For one thing, there are three preconditions for the identification of a culture: the group of relics and remains should belong to the same era, be distributed in the same area, and show the same characteristics. For example, if a group of specific objects is found frequently in a certain type of dwelling places or tombs of a certain area, this combination of remains and relics can be called a "culture". The group of excavated relics at Hemudu could certainly meet the preconditions. For another, most cultures are named after the specific places where the typical site was first discovered, such as Mousterian, Solutrean, Magdalenian in Europe, and Zhoukoudian (周口店), Dingcun (丁村), Xiaonanhai (小南海), Yangshao (仰韶), and Dawenkou (大汶口) in China. Therefore, the Hemudu culture was likewise named after its place of discovery — Hemudu Village.

Hemudu used to be an ancient ferry on the Yuyao River. The name has gone through some changes. Till the late Qing Dynasty, it was called "Huangmudu"[1] (黄墓渡), which could be proved by the tablet in the pavilion on the north bank of the ferry, erected in 1786, the 51st year of Emperor

---

[1] The name "Huangmudu" (黄墓渡) means "the ferry-place near the tomb of the revered Mr. Huang."

Qianlong's (乾隆) reign. There is a legend about the origin of the name "Huangmudu". According to "The Story of Marquis Liu" (" 留侯世家 ") in *Shiji* (《史记》, *Records of the Grand Historian*), during the vicissitude of Qin and Han Dynasties, a famous scholar — Cui Guang (崔广), and three other famous recluses lived in solitude in the Shangshan Mountain (商山). They were all in their 80s, with white hair but ruddy complexion, thus known as "the Four White-heads in the Shangshan Mountain". Later, Empress Lü (吕后) figured out a scheme and "invited" them to the palace to assist Liu Ying (刘盈), the crown prince, in the battle for the throne. Finally, Liu Ying came to the throne as the second emperor of the Han Dynasty after the death of Emporer Gaozu, Liu Bang (刘邦). But Lü, then Empress Dowager, grabbed all the power in the actual reign. Dissatisfied with this, Cui changed his name to Huang Gong (黄公) and fled to the east of Yong (甬，Ningbo in brief). Legend has it that he lived in seclusion in the mountains near Hemudu and died of old age. Huang Zongxi (黄宗羲), a historian in the early Qing Dynasty, explored Huang Gong's burial place in *A Record of the Siming Mountains*, noting that "Huang Gong was buried in a mountain named Fuchuan (覆船，Overturned Boat) along a river". This mountain, located on the south bank of the ferry, is now named the Dutou Mountain (渡头山，the Ferry Mountain) and known as the Yuanbao Mountain (元宝山，the Silver Ingot Mountain) among the local people. As the nearby villagers thought the name "Fuchuan" unlucky, especially for people making a living by fishing and ferry, the homophone "Fuquan" (福泉，Happiness Spring) gradually took the place of the ominous "Fuchuan". Up to now, on the south bank of the ferry, at the junction where the Zhilin Creek (芝林溪) flows into Yuyao River, still stands a single-arch stone bridge with "Fuquan Bridge" (福泉桥) on it. Ethnologists tend to believe that "Huangmudu" is gradually changed into "Hemudu" because of an error in its spreading in the local dialect, for the two names were pronounced similarly. Compiled during the reign of Emperor Kangxi (康熙), *Chronicles of Lushan Temple* (《芦山寺志》) says: "People are mistaken, calling 'Huangmudu' by 'Hemudu'." It seems that in the early Qing Dynasty, it was already called "Hemudu" among the illiterate villagers in the surrounding countryside. The written form "Huangmudu" was only known to scholars. The village called Hemu on the south bank of the ferry also lends credence to this opinion .

Though the two archeological excavations mapped out the features and stages of the Hemudu culture, a single tree cannot make a forest. As far as the archeological culture is concerned, a single site of Hemudu was obviously not enough, and most importantly, the distribution range of this culture still needed to be ascertained. Therefore, from 1979 to 1980, the cultural relics departments in Zhejiang Province began an archeological survey of the distribution of the Hemudu culture, centering on the banks of the Yuyao River. After some hard work, a total of more than 30 sites of the Hemudu culture were discovered, and the distribution of the Hemudu culture was roughly defined.

In the 1980s, the archeological excavation of the Hemudu culture suspended for a while, and in-depth research was carried out, focusing on the collation and digesting of the archeological data. Experts from different disciplines published research papers in various professional journals, further promoting and expanding the influence of the Hemudu culture at home and abroad. They covered various topics: the dating of the Hemudu Site, the identification of the species of the excavated rice, animals, and plants, its ancient environment and climate, water transportation, primitive art and music, farming tools, livestock raising, house construction technology, and the identification of wells. The experts discussed the aspects such as the cultural connotation of the Hemudu culture, the protection of its wooden cultural relics, its relationship with the ancient Yue people (越人), and its influence on Japan. In August 2003, the pamphlet *Hemudu—Archeology and Excavation Report of Sites in the Neolithic Age* (《河姆渡——新石器时代遗址考古发掘报告 》) was published by Cultural Relics Press, and consolidated the research results of the Hemudu culture over the years.

Though the discovery and the establishment of the Hemudu culture was one of the breakthroughs in the research of Neolithic prehistory in China in the 1970s, and a milestone in this field, there were still some unanswered questions and unsolved problems. For instance, the connotation of the Hemudu culture was not yet completely presented by only the Hemudu Site itself; there was an obvious cultural gap between the second and third phases; the distribution range was not quite clear; the layout pattern of settlement was not clear, and not a site was found with the coexistence of a village residence and other settlement elements like burials; there were still doubts about the structures, units, and techniques of wooden stilt houses; the origin and successor of the Hemudu culture were still unknown; and the social patterns of the Hemudu culture were yet to be explored. For these reasons, in the 1980s, the Zhejiang Provincial Cultural Relics and Archeological Institute set up the "Hemudu Culture Research Group" to carry out further research on the Hemudu culture. After more than thirty years of excavations and research, archeologists have basically clarified the distribution range and the connotation of the Hemudu culture, filled in the missing links in the development of the Hemudu culture, and found the successor culture of the Hemudu culture. The achievements of this phase of research were mainly gained from the trial excavations and excavations of the following prehistoric sites in Ningbo.

About 8 kilometers northeast of the Hemudu Site, in the northwest corner of Cicheng Town (慈城镇), Jiangbei District, Ningbo City, lies the Cihu Site (慈湖遗址), with an existing area of about 2,000 square meters. Two excavations in 1986 and 1988, covering an area of about 300 square meters, yielded hundreds of artifacts made of stone, bone, wood, and pottery, as well as a small number of plant remains such as jujubes (酸枣). In particular, the discovery of many wooden production tools and utensils enriched the content of the Hemudu culture. The 21-meter-thick culture deposits were divided into two layers. The lower layer shows the characteristics of the late phase of the Hemudu culture. The upper layer has the characteristics of the Liangzhu culture (良渚文化) in addition to those of its own, suggesting a new cultural connotation in the development of the Hemudu culture into the Liangzhu culture in the Ningbo area. This new cultural connotation has not only filled the missing link in the development of the Hemudu culture, but also confirmed the existence of the layer of the Liangzhu culture in the Ningbo-Shaoxing Plain (宁绍平原) for the first time.

Then, the Mingshanhou Site (名山后遗址) was discovered in Mingshanhou Village (名山后村), Nanpu Town (南浦乡), Fenghua District[①], Ningbo City, covering a total area of about 20,000 square meters. An area of 360 square meters was excavated in 1989 and 1991. The 2.7-meter-thick cultural deposits were divided into 12 layers. The eighth layer and below are equivalent to the third period of the Hemudu culture. The second to seventh layers belong to the Liangzhu culture. The excavation of the Mingshanhou Site provided substantial material for the study of the follow-on developments of the Hemudu culture, and indicated the clearest superimposition of culture layers belonging to the Hemudu culture and the Liangzhu culture .

In 1990 and 1992, excavations were carried out in the Tashan Site (塔山 遗址) at the southern foot of the Tashan Mountain in the eastern suburb of Dancheng Town (丹城镇), Xiangshan County. The Tashan Site covered a total area of about 10,000 square meters. The first two excavations covered 545 square meters, and several further excavations have been carried out since 2007. The 2.8-meter-thick cultural deposits were divided into 9 layers, among which three layers belong to the Neolithic Age, with the lower and middle layers equivalent to the third and fourth phases of the Hemudu culture respectively, and the upper layer equivalent to the Liangzhu culture. The clan cemetery (氏族墓地) of the Hemudu culture was excavated for the first time in the lower layer. In the upper layer, typical ware of the Liangzhu culture were unearthed, such as basin-shaped tripods (鼎), jars with two

---

①   Fenghua used to be a county. In 1988, it was upgraded to a county level city. In 2016, it became a district under the municipality of Ningbo. 历史沿革 [EB/OL]. [2022-01-20]. http://www.fh.gov.cn/art/2020/5/26/art_1229045103_43485702.html.

lugs, and *dou* (豆， stemmed bowl) with bamboo-shaped handles (竹节把 豆). The cultural layers marked 4-B, 4-A, and 3, and remains units coded H2 and H23 belong to the Shang and Zhou Dynasties. The tombs excavated in the Tashan Site provide abundant research material for the study of the social structure and burial customs in the later phase of the Hemudu culture.

The Xiaodongmen Site (小东门遗址), covering an area of 400 square meters now, is located at the southeastern foot of the Tangshan Mountain (汤 山), outside the Xiaodongmen Gate (小东门) of Cicheng Town, Jiangbei District, 8 kilometers northeast of the Hemudu Site. In 1992, an area of about 200 square meters was excavated. The cultural deposits, 1.8 to 3 meters thick, were divided into 9 cultural layers, of which the sixth, seventh and eighth layers and the burials under the fifth layer belong to the first phase of this culture, corresponding to the third phase of the Hemudu culture. The fourth and fifth layers belong to the second phase of this culture, equivalent to the Liangzhu culture. The third layer and the remains of the pillar cave with an opening beneath the third layer belong to the third phase of this culture, corresponding to the Maqiao culture (马桥文化), the late phase of the Liangzhu culture. The second layer is the fourth phase of this culture, with excavated artifacts showing widely varied styles, some featuring the Maqiao culture, and others bearing the characteristics of the early Spring and Autumn Period. This suggests that remains of the fourth phase might have been disturbed by human activities. This excavation has provided physical materials for the in-depth study of the Hemudu culture, the Liangzhu culture, and the culture of the Shang and Zhou Dynasties.

The Xiangjiashan Site (鲞架山遗址) is located at the southeast foot of the Xiangjiashan Mountain, Lushansi Village (芦山寺村), Hemudu Town, Yuyao County. It covers a total area of about 20,000 square meters and is only 1 kilometer northeast of the Hemudu Site. The excavation was divided into two areas: A and B. The cultural deposits are 2 meters thick. The Neolithic Age deposits are further divided into three phases: the fourth layer constitutes the first phase, corresponding to the time between the third and second phases of the Hemudu culture; the 5 urn burials (瓮棺葬) in Area A belong to the second phase, corresponding to the early fourth phase of the Hemudu culture; the ash pits with openings beneath the second and third layers in Area B belong to the third phase, corresponding to the late fourth phase of the Hemudu culture. The fourth phase of this culture only exists in the second layer and units H3 and H14, with stamped hard pottery (印纹硬陶) and proto-porcelain as the majority of the relics unearthed, which can be dated from the late Spring and Autumn Period to the early Warring States Period. The sintered clay altar (红烧土祭台) reflects the spiritual life of the Hemudu people (河姆渡先民). The excavation of the Xiangjiashan Site has filled the gap between the second and third phases of the Hemudu culture and enriched its cultural connotation, making the evolutionary trajectory of the Hemudu culture more complete.

The Zishan Site (鲻山遗址) lies at the southern foot of the Zishan Mountain, Huitou Village (汇头村), Zhangting Town (丈亭镇), Yuyao County, more than 10 kilometers northwest of the Hemudu Site, covering a total area of about 50,000 square meters. In 1996, an area of 306 square meters was excavated. The 3-meter-thick culture deposits can be divided into 10 layers, involving the Hemudu culture, the Liangzhu culture, and the Stamped Pottery culture (印纹陶文化) in the Shang and Zhou Dynasties. In the lower part of the second layer exist the Shang and Zhou cultural deposits, and also two tombs of the Liangzhu culture. The third to tenth layers are the Hemudu culture deposits, which can be divided into four phases: Layers 10 and 9 belong to the late stage of the first phase of the Hemudu culture; layer 8 corresponds to the early stage of its second phase; layers 6 and 7 correspond to the late stage of its second phase; layers 3, 4 and 5 are equivalent to its third phase. Around a thousand pieces of stone tools, bone (horn, tooth) implements, woodwork, and pottery were excavated. The remains of wooden constructions and animal and plant remains like rice and tortoiseshells were discovered. A batch of small stone tools made of flint was also excavated from the site, which enriched the connotation of the Hemudu culture. This excavation provides new data for the study of the wooden stilt houses and the settlement form of the Hemudu culture.

The Fujiashan Site (傅家山遗址) is located at the foot of Fujiashan Mountain, Baziqiao Village (八字桥村), Cicheng Town, Yuyao County, more than 10 kilometers northeast of the Hemudu Site, covering an area of about 2,000 square meters. In 2004, a rescue excavation was carried out before the construction of the south connecting section of Hangzhou Bay Bridge in this area, covering an area of 725 square meters. The culture deposits can be divided into 8 layers. The seventh layer and the eighth layer are the deposits of the Hemudu culture. The relics of stilt buildings and ash pits in the early period of the Hemudu culture were found. More than 570 intact or recoverable artifacts were unearthed, including artifacts made of jade, stone, bone, pottery, and wood, which could be divided into three categories: production tools, utensils, and carved artworks. There were also some fruits, seeds, and animal bones. The Fujiashan Site is a Neolithic village site with various economic forms such as fishing and hunting, gathering, and farming. It is another important discovery of the early Hemudu culture in the Yuyao River Region after the discovery of the Hemudu Site.

The Tongjia'ao Site (童家岙遗址) is located in the north of Tong'ao Village (童岙村), Henghe Town (横河镇), Cixi County, in the fields in the northeast of Dabutou Village (大埠头村). It is more than 20 kilometers away from the Hemudu Site in the northwest, with a total area of over 20,000 square meters. In 1979 and 2009, drilling and trial excavations were carried out on the site respectively, and remains of roads and stilt houses were found. The deposits formed four successive phases: T1 (layers 4 and 5), T2 (layer 9) and T3 (layer 8) belong to the first phase; T2 (layers 8) and T3 (layers 6 and 7) belong to the second phase; T1 (layers 2A, 2B and layer 3) belongs to the third phase; T2 (layers 6 and 7) and T3 (layer 4) belong to the fourth phase, corresponding to the fourth phase of the Hemudu culture.

The Tianluoshan Site (田螺山遗址) is located in Xiang'ao Village (相岙村), Sanqishi Town (三七市镇), Yuyao County, about 7 kilometers northeast of the Hemudu Site, with a total area of more than 30,000 square meters. The culture deposits are divided into 6 cultural layers. The thickest part has a depth of more than 3 meters. Through years of continuous excavations since 2004, more than 1,200 square meters of residential areas and more than 1,000 square meters of ancient rice farming areas have been excavated. The excavations have revealed multiple-level stilt houses, burials, food storage pits, roads, wood bridges, wood fortress walls, and ancient rice farming remains, over 5,000 artifacts of pottery, stone (jade), bone (horn and tooth) and wood, as well as numerous remains of animal bones, grain husks, charred rice grains, water chestnuts, acorns (橡子), and gourds. The Tianluoshan Site is the best-preserved ancient village site of the Hemudu culture discovered so far, in terms of the surface environment and underground remains.

The study on the Tianluoshan Site is characterized by meticulous archeological excavation and multidisciplinary research, marking a new stage in the Hemudu culture research. In the archeological excavations, each cultural layer was further divided into 3 sub-layers, and soil samples were collected for quantitative analysis from 7 different parts of each trial pit for all sub-layers before the water sieving and flotation, and then the materials contained were manually sorted out. As a result, many small artifacts unseen before were found. Another feature of the excavations at the Tianluoshan Site was the involvement of dozens of experts and scholars of different disciplines who came from countries like the United States, Britain, France, Australia, the Republic of Korea, and Japan. Various advanced methods and technologies in natural sciences were used, which greatly expanded the depth and breadth of the archeological research. In the exploration of the environment of the Hemudu culture, various methods were employed, for instance, the carbon-14 dating of annual reeds and acorns, the identification of plant seeds and mammalian species, the analysis of diatoms (硅藻), pollen, and parasite eggs, the study on pharyngeal bones in fish-bone pits, the determination of carbon and nitrogen isotope composition of human and animal bones, as well as the observation of the soil in terms of its grain size, the magnetic susceptibility, the clay mineral composition, and the variation in boron content, paleosalinity, and phytolith content. The findings of these studies have been compiled and published under the title *An Integrative Study on the Tianluoshan Ecofacts*[1]. In addition, there were studies on the composition of stone tools and the origin of stone materials of the tools, the identification and analysis of the surface residues on artifacts of stone, wood, and pottery, the experimental archeological study of the bone *si*, and the conservation of soil in the cultural layers and wood tools.

It has been almost forty years since the discovery of the Hemudu culture, and its cultural connotation, distribution range, and chronological phasing have basically been clarified. Meanwhile, rich information has been collected for the reconstruction of the production and life of the Hemudu ancients.

More than 7,000 years ago, the Hemudu ancients had already emerged from the barbaric raw-meat-eating lifestyle and started a settled life. The villages, located by the rolling Siming Mountains or the Cinan Hills (慈南 山地), were relatively small in scale, less than 50,000 square meters each. At the outskirts of the villages, a wooden wall, consisting of 2 or 3 rows of closely arranged piles, was built to mark the village boundary and guard against ferocious wild animals, poisonous snakes and insects. A number of wood or bamboo gates were made embedded in the wall; the river outside the village was bridged with a log; the roads were built on a base of wood piles, some even with reed mats or reed stalks inside for reinforcement, and paved with pellets of sintered earth, twigs, and broken pottery pieces. The houses in the village were all arranged with hills at their backs and waters in the front. The earliest houses were built on rows of stilts driven into the earth as the foundation, on which keels were laid to support the floor, forming an elevated building base. Then columns (柱) and beams (梁) were erected upon the floor with the roof on top. A ladder made of a log was used to

---

①   It was published by Cultural Relics Press in 2011.

access the house. The structure, more than 23 meters long, 7 meters deep, with a 1.3-meter-wide front porch, was a longhouse accommodating many people. Such stilt houses were adapted to the damp and rainy environment of the area, and protected people from the attacks of wild animals. Today stilt houses still exist in Southeast Asia and the minority areas of Yunnan Province in China. In addition to tying the wooden timbers when building houses, mortise-and-tenon work was also used at some of the vertically intersecting nodes. The types of mortise-and-tenon joints include head tenons （ 榫) and foot tenons on the column (柱头柱脚榫), tenons at the end of the beam （ 梁头榫) , tenons with dowel holes, tenons with mortises (带卯眼榫), dovetail joints (燕尾榫), middle column mortises (平身柱卯眼), corner pillar mortises (转角柱卯眼), lattice railing mortises (直棂栏杆卯眼), rabbet joints (企口板) and carved wood components (刻花木构件). These wood structures were finely processed in accordance with the mechanic sprinciples. This discovery suggests the history of the tenon-and-mortise work (榫卯技术) in China was more than 3,000 years earlier than previously thought, and proved the Hemudu culture as an important starting place of Chinese traditional tenon-and-mortise technique (中国传统榫卯木构建筑技术). In the middle phase of the culture, the house building technique evolved concerning the treatment of the pillars. First, rectangular pillar pits were dug with tools like bone *si*, and then round or square wood pillars were erected in the pits. Later, the method developed into padding the pillar pits with a plate at the bottom before erecting the pillars. The plate at the bottom, an original form of the column base, would prevent the pillar from sinking under the weight on it. In the late phase of the Hemudu culture, in addition to stilt buildings, there were also ground buildings resting on piles of materials. The pillar foundation was built with red burned clay, clay, and broken pottery pieces layer by layer for consolidation, and looked like an inverted "steel helmet". Sometimes people simply used boulders as the pillar foundations. The walls were reinforced with reeds, plastered both on the inside and the outside, and the interior space began to be separated by earth walls. The inside surface of the wall was fired to form a layer of burned clay 1–2 centimeters thick, and some of them were even paved with broken pottery pieces. Hearth pits (灶坑) were dug into the indoor ground for cooking.

Primitive people used to live and be buried in groups. But in the cultural layers of the early period of the Hemudu culture, no public clan cemetery was found. Only a pottery *fu* (釜 , cauldron) and a pottery pot containing the remains of fish bones and so on were found. Later, burials scattered around the houses were excavated, with no pits or burial utensils, and most of them had no burial objects. Single burials with bent limbs on their sides were popular. The human bones were well preserved, but the skull or limbs were mostly incomplete, and most of them were under age, mostly infants and children. It was presumed to be a special burial form for those who died unnaturally. In the late phase of the culture, there were still scattered graves for unnatural deaths around the houses, with no burial utensils or few burial objects. The human bones were poorly preserved, with upright limbs, many with incomplete skulls or limbs, and generally buried in rectangular vertical pits dug into the ground. At the Tashan Site, a clan cemetery for group burials was found, with more than 50 tombs, mostly shaft tombs. They are divided into two types: primary burials and secondary burials. For the primary burial, the dead were laid facing up with straight limbs. For the secondary burial, most of the skeletons were generally arranged in the original state (facing up with straight limbs), but some were laid in random piles. The burial objects were mainly pottery and a small number of decorative jade — *jue* (玦). At the Xiangjiashan Site, collective "urn burials" were found around a platform made of red burned clay, with charcoal scraps and white fragments of burned bones scattered on the platform and around the urn coffins.

Rice was the staple food for the Hemudu people. In the two excavations of the Hemudu Site, a large amount of rice was found. Such a quantity and distribution area of rice has not been seen at other sites. When first unearthed, it was still bright yellow in color and intact in shape, even with clearly discernible veins and glume hairs. According to features, such as the average length, the width of the glume and the distribution of paleae on the glume, the excavated rice belonged to the cultivated subspecies named *Oryza Sativa L. subsp hsien Ting* (籼亚种中晚稻型水稻). Further identification suggested that what was excavated was a mixture of rice species cultivated in Asia with obvious variation in grain sizes, mainly indica rice (籼稻), followed by japonica rice (粳稻), and some transitional species. In addition, wild rice grains were also identified with scanning electron microscopes, indicating that the Hemudu people also collected wild rice while farming rice. In recent years, the excavation of the Tianluoshan Site revealed deposits of rice husks, rice stalks, and rice leaves. Intact rice grains and a large number of carbonized rice grains were also found in the Tianluoshan Site, while in other sites, only hulled rice grains were found instead of grains with husks. This indicated that rice cultivation was a very common phenomenon then among the Hemudu people. Furthermore, a set of tools that functioned in all the processes from rice farming to shucking were found. The bone *si* was the most characteristic production tool of the Hemudu culture. More than 170 pieces were unearthed at the Hemudu Site alone, and many were found at other sites such as Tianluoshan, Tongjia'ao and Zishan as well. The bone *si* retained the natural shape of the shoulder blades of deer, buffaloes, and other big animals, from which they had been made. Archeologists used the shoulder blades of modern buffaloes to simulate the bone *si* and carried out experiments with the simulated ones. The reconstructed bone *si* looked like today's shovels, suitable for shoveling and digging. The results showed that the bone *si* was an important agricultural production tool for ancient people, fully capable of removing reed weeds, ditching, digging holes, and plowing farmland. The wood *si* was made afterwards, replacing the bone *si* as the main farming tool. The ancient people planted rice on the low-lying marshland by lakes, without square paddies or water conservancy facilities like ditches and water-storage wells. In order to walk in and out of the field conveniently, the ancients paved some ridges in the paddy fields with branches. According to the drilling survey results at the Hemudu Site and the Tianluoshan Site, the size of paddy fields owned by each village was about 100 *mu* (亩 , 1 *mu* equals 0.0667 hectares or 666.67 square meters). It was generally believed bone sickles were the harvest tools, which is in fact a guess of the past based on the present. However, bone sickles are also used for leather kneading in some minority areas. It was stone knives (石刀) or bone knives made from wild boar tusks that might have been used to harvest rice by the Hemudu people. Wooden pestles, grinding plates, and grinding sticks were tools to hull rice.

In addition to rice, the Hemudu people might have also cultivated gourds and tea. Well-preserved gourds and gourd seeds, which could have been planted artificially, were often found in archeological excavations, still brightly colored when first unearthed. Surprisingly, clumps of plant roots, found in both of the two shallow pits dug by ancients at the Tianluoshan Site, were identified as those of the genus Camellia (山茶属). When these roots were soaked in water, a lot of tea polyphenols (茶多酚) could be released. The Hemudu ancients seemed to have started artificial tea planting and tea drinking as early as six or seven thousand years ago.

Pigs and dogs were domesticated by the Hemudu people. The skull of the pig had a wider head and a shorter snout, which was obviously different from that of a wild boar. There was a fat pottery pig with a drooping abdomen, short limbs, and a 1 : 1 front-rear proportion. Its shape was similar to that of modern pigs, indicating that pigs had been domesticated for quite a long time. The skulls of dogs were relatively intact, and completely different from the way ancient people treated other animals. A lot of dog excrement was found near the houses, containing things like fish bones. It suggested a relatively close relationship between humans and dogs back then and constituted direct evidence of dogs as livestock. Remains of buffaloes were also unearthed, which were short-horned water buffaloes (*Bubalus Mephistopheles*), to be exact. They had been thought to be artificially raised as livestock before, but it was held after reappraisals that evidence of domestication was not sufficient and that they might have been obtained in hunting.

Gathering, fishing, and hunting were important auxiliary economies of the Hemudu people. To supplement their food needs, they collected water chestnuts, Gorgon fruit (芡实), and lotus roots (藕) from shallow ponds and lakes, as well as wild fruits like acorns, peaches, plums, jujubes, and wild grapes from forests in the surrounding mountains. Many circular and rectangular pits were found near the houses for their storage. The bottom of the pits was often paved with reed mats. Although the plant species of their collection covered a wide variety, the majority are acorns, water chestnuts, and Gorgon fruit; others are few in number.

All kinds of broken animal bones were scattered around the settlement, casually discarded by the ancients after they had cracked the bones and sucked the marrow, some being the scraps left from tool making as well. According to rough identification, the animal remains unearthed at the Hemudu Site belonged to 61 species, the majority being deer, fish, tortoises, and soft-shelled turtles, which might have been the main prey in their fishing and hunting. It is worth noting that all the monkey skulls excavated from the Hemudu culture were broken and showed traces of deliberate cracking, which, according to experts' speculation, is related to their habit of eating monkey brains. Numerous fishing and hunting tools were excavated, including bone arrowheads, bone whistles, bone fish darts (骨鱼镖), stone balls (石球), stone pellets (石丸), and wooden oars. Bone arrowheads of all shapes, in particular, made up the majority of the artifacts unearthed. At the Tianluoshan Site, bone arrowheads accounted for almost half of all the excavated artifacts. It was a good indication of the development of fishing and hunting at that time.

Apart from meat and hides of the hunted animals, various parts of animal bones were also made full use of, which, after grinding and processing, they were made into all kinds of artifacts widely used in agricultural production, hunting and fishing, weaving and sewing, as well as human body decoration and artworks. The wide variety of bone tools is one of the most remarkable features of the Hemudu culture.

The earliest wooden wells (木构水井) in China to date were found in the Hemudu culture. Well digging was a major innovation of humans' cognition, exploiting and transformation of nature, and had an invaluable impact on human life. Wells provided clean water for domestic use, and were later used for irrigation and pottery making, thus reducing humanity's dependence on nature and creating conditions for the exploitation of areas without adequate surface water.

Among the early production tools bone (horn and tooth) and wood tools constituted the majority for their great numbers and varieties, while stone tools accounted for only a small proportion. The stone tools included only axes, adzes, chisels, and grindstones (砺石). They were hard, small, and roughly processed, with only the edges finely honed and traces of chipping still left on the rest parts of the tools. They were mainly used for felling trees, processing wood components, and making wooden tools. The stone axes (石斧) and stone adzes (石锛) were bound with wooden or horn handles as composite tools, and greatly improved labor efficiency. Grindstones made of finer red sandstone must have been used to polish bone and wooden tools, as deep grooves were often left on their surface. The variety of stone tools increased in the later period of the culture, including axes, adzes, chisels, knives, spindle whorls, grinding balls, grindstones, as well as several rough stone scythes (石镰) and a new type of perforated stone axes. The stone used was softer than before, and the processing was finer, resulting in a regular shape and a well-polished surface. Most of them were still tools for carpentry work. Some of the larger grindstones had a wider and smoother grinding surface, which were probably millstones, used in conjunction with stone grinding balls (石磨盘).

The variety and number of bone tools far surpassed those of other materials. The Hemudu culture was characterized by the production and use of a large number of bone, horn, and tooth tools. Bone tools such as *si*, arrowheads, whistles, awls, chisels, daggers, needles, darts, handles, and shuttle-shaped tools were widely used in all types of production, like agriculture, weaving, hunting, and woodworking.

Wooden tools had a wide range of uses. In addition to the wooden *si* (木 耜), there were also seed dibbles (点种棒) with one or both ends made into rounded tips, handles of all shapes, shovels, swords, hoes, mallets, pestles, arrowheads, and paddles, as well as the cloth roller and weft beaters, which probably had been part of primitive weaving machines.

The variety of pottery production tools was limited, including only a small number of pottery spindle whorls (陶纺轮), pottery pellets, and pottery paddles (陶拍).

The majority of utensils for daily use were pottery. In the early period, charcoal-tempered pottery was the mainstay. Its making process was worth noting: first mix charred plant stems, leaves, and grain husks with sericite clay, then shape the clay by hand, and finally fire the green-ware at about 850 °C. Such pottery ware had many shortcomings, like low hardness, loose texture, and high water absorption; moreover, the hand-made pottery ware always had thick walls, irregular shapes, and even skewed and twisted forms. The surface of the vessels was always decorated, mainly with cord patterns and incised floral motifs, a small number of them embossed with animal designs or painted in various colors. As the types of foot are concerned, there were flat-footed vessels, round-footed vessels, and ring-footed vessels, but no three-legged vessels. In terms of the forms, there were *fu*, jars, basins, trays, *bo* (钵, bowl), cauldron supports, lids, and a small number of *yu* (盂, jar), *he* (盉, pitcher), and *dou*. In the late period of the Hemudu culture, the number of charcoal-tempered pottery vessels decreased significantly, while sand-tempered pottery vessels became more popular and clay pottery (泥质陶) ones came into being. All the charcoal-tempered pottery was polished and treated with a red coat. Pottery decoration was greatly reduced, with the cord pattern as the mainstay, mostly found on *fu*, tripods, and other cookware. There were also incised patterns, additional modeling, and open work decorations. The shape of the vessels became regular, as slow-wheels were adopted during the adjustment of the hand-made green-ware. There was a full range of round-footed, flat-footed, three-legged and ring-footed vessels. Various ware like *fu*, tripods, *dou*, jars, basins, plates, *bo*, *gui* (鬶, tripod with three hollow legs), *he*, mortars, cauldron supports, and lids have been unearthed.

Daily utensils made of tooth, horn, and bone were fewer, with only bone spoons (骨匙) excavated. Domestic utensils like lacquered bowls (漆碗), basins, plates, bottles, and spoons were made of wood.

Body ornaments such as jade pieces like *jue* and *huang* (璜, pendant)[1], stone beads, bone hairpins, and other ornaments made of tooth and horn have been excavated.

In addition, there were a large number of finely crafted bird-shaped or butterfly-shaped vessels of various sizes made of stone, wood, bone, and ivory. The ivory ones were the most exquisite, with intricate carvings on the front, the most common motifs being birds and sun patterns. The birds and sun patterns reflected the Hemudu people' sun worshiping and bird worshiping. And the wooden bird-shaped vessels (鸟形器) were generally painted with lacquer or lacquer floral motifs. Wooden cylinders (筒), found in large numbers, were also special objects discovered exclusively in the Hemudu culture. They were found in large numbers and shaped like hollow bamboo cylinders, with a partition and wooden cakes inside. Some were painted with black lacquer on the outside and tied with rattan at both ends, whose function is unknown yet. There were also a small number of pottery sculptures like pigs and sheep, as well as pottery toys and wood tops.

The Hemudu culture is one of the most important Neolithic cultures in the Yangtze River Region. According to the carbon-14 dating, it existed from about 7,000 years ago to 5,300 years ago. During the more than 1,700 years of its existence, all the aspects of production and life went through constant development. In archeology, when a culture develops into an apparently

---

[1] The jade pieces are named after its shape. *Jue* is made by binding two pieces of jade into one and *huang* is a piece of jade shaped in a semi-circle.

different type, it can be called a new phase (or period) of the same culture. But if it undergoes a qualitative change, it should be considered as another culture. The Hemudu Site is a typical site of the Hemudu culture, with four cultural layers superimposed on each other and the layers basically successive in age. Although the excavated artifacts from each layer were distinctive, they were far from being qualitatively different, and many cultural factors were present throughout the four layers consistently. Therefore, the four cultural layers represent four different stages of the Hemudu culture, rather than four different cultures. Archeologists have synthesized the existing archeological findings of the Hemudu culture and divided it into four major phases, each subdivided into the early and late stages, making a total of four phases and eight stages within the frame of the Hemudu culture.

The Hemudu culture was a Neolithic culture distributed mainly in Ningbo. Only five sites in its early phase (7,000 to 6,000 years ago) have been found, namely Hemudu, Zishan, Tianluoshan, Fujiashan, and Tongjia'ao. They were concentrated at the foot of mountains around Yuyao-Cicheng Plain, located in the Yuyao River Valley (姚江谷地). The area spans 10 kilometers from north to south and over 20 kilometers from east to west. About 6,000 years ago, the number of sites soared to more than 30, and the distribution range was significantly expanded. The Hemudu ancients began to move out of the Yuyao River Valley. Eastwards, they went to the Sanjiang Plain (三江平原) and even crossed the sea to the Zhoushan Islands; southwards, they arrived at the Yinzhou-Fenghua Plain (鄞奉平原), Xiangshan Peninsula (象山半岛), and the farthest place — Taizhou City; westwards, they crossed the Cao'e River (曹娥江) and arrived in Shaoxing City. But most sites are still concentrated in the Yuyao-Cicheng Plain (余慈平原), especially in the near foothills of the Siming Mountains and the mountainous region south of Cixi County, forming a strip of settlements. Due to changes in the natural environment, the hinterland of the plains, previously unsuitable for human life, was also gradually populated.

The discovery and recognition of the Hemudu culture is a major breakthrough in Neolithic archeology in China, proving that the Yangtze River Region was also one of the birthplaces of the Chinese people, like the Yellow River Region. Its significance can be summed up in the following aspects.

1. The Rewriting of the History of Ancient Chinese Civilizations

The abundance of historic texts proves that the Chinese attach great importance to history. But the "Twenty-four Histories"[1] record and present only the history of dynastic changes centered on the Yellow River Valley. From these historic documents, modern historians, both Chinese and foreign, once concluded that the Yellow River Valley was the cradle of the Chinese people, while other regions were settled by uncivilized barbarians.

But in 1973, the discovery and excavation of the Hemudu Site revealed large areas of rice remains and mortise-and-tenon-jointed timberwork buildings, charming ivory carvings, and exquisite lacquered woodwork, as well as charcoal-tempered pottery like *fu*, jars, pots, plates, and *bo*. The unique cultural landscape and its existence more than 7,000 years ago determined by the carbon-14 dating shocked the archeological and historic community at the time, thus challenging the belief that Chinese civilization originated in the Yellow River Region. Since then, the academic circle has unanimously agreed that both the Yangtze River Region and the Yellow River Region are the birthplaces of ancient civilizations in China, and the Hemudu Site in the south, together with the Banpo Site (半坡遗址) in Xi'an in the north, has been recorded in history books. Its important status and contribution to the development of ancient Chinese civilizations have never been challenged, even when new archeological discoveries of cultural sites have been made in China, many of which existed earlier than Hemudu, for the subsequent discoveries only add quantitative evidence to this view, instead of developing it qualitatively. Therefore, Hemudu has been reputed to be one of the most important sites in the history of China since its discovery.

---

[1]　The "Twenty-four Histories" is the collective name for the 24 ancient Chinese chronicles of the dynasties, arranged in the successive order.

2. The Starting Point for the Research on the Origins of Rice Farming

Rice was one of the first food crops to be domesticated and cultivated by man, and is also the world's most important food crop. Today, nearly one-third of the world's population rely on rice as the staple food. The discovery of cultivated rice in the Hemudu culture, the abundant remains of rice farming, and the associated tools for rice cultivating, harvesting, and processing, indicated that the Hemudu people had already gone through a rather long experimenting period of rice farming. Mr. Chen Wenhua[1] (陈文华) pointed out in the preface to *A Preliminary Exploration of the Hemudu Culture* (《 河姆渡文化初探 》), "The cultural remains of rice farming at the Hemudu Site suggested it was the oldest and richest rice culture (稻作文化) in the world at that time. Since the origin of rice farming has been one of the most important archeological topics in world agriculture, the Hemudu culture has inevitably attracted the attention of scholars studying the origins of Asian civilization. In the past decade or so, the word 'Hemudu' has become almost synonymous with Chinese rice culture. Although rice farming sites older than the Hemudu Site will be found in the future, the Hemudu Site will remain a glorious milestone, and its historical status and scientific value are unshakable."[2] Mr. Chen's prediction has been affirmed today. At present, the remains of rice cultivation dating from a time earlier than the Hemudu culture have been found at the Shangshan Site (上山遗址) in Pujiang County, Zhejiang Province and the Xiaohuangshan Site (小黄山遗址) in Shengzhou County, Zhejiang Province. There are many more such remains outside Zhejiang Province, such as the Xianrendong Cave Site and the Diaotonghuan Cave Site (仙人洞与吊桶环遗址) in Wannian County, Jiangxi Province, where rice phytolith of 10,000 years old was found. The discovery of 10,000-year-old rice at the Yuchanyan Cave Site (玉蟾岩洞穴遗址) in Hunan Province has pushed the upper limit of rice agriculture in China to the Early Neolithic Period about 10,000 years ago.

---

①   Chen Wenhua (1935–2014) was a famous expert in agricultural archeology in China.

②   林华东 . 河姆渡文化初探 [M]. 杭州：浙江人民出版社，1992.

In the above-mentioned sites, the scarcity of material and the complexity of the situation made the application of many identification tools difficult. Although the rice culture at Hemudu began several thousand years later, the abundance of rice, the associated farming, harvesting, and processing tools, and the cooking and dining utensils formed a complete evidence chain. Thus a unanimous agreement has been achieved at home and abroad that the rice at Hemudu was artificially cultivated; and the rice at Hemudu has become a benchmark for the study of the origins of rice farming, against which any newly found rice remains will be examined to determine its status as a wild or domesticated species. Thus, the Hemudu culture has become the starting point for the study of rice farming.

The beginning of rice farming is epoch-making in human history. However, the academic community is divided as to where rice farming originated. Two types of rice are cultivated in the world, namely Asian rice (亚洲稻 , *Oryza sativa*) and African rice (*Oryza glaberrima*). Asian rice was domesticated from a perennial Asian wild rice and originated in the tropical and subtropical regions of Asia. Now it has been the rice species most often planted around the world. African rice is only found in parts of West Africa and some areas of Central and South America. For this reason, the origin of cultivated rice in Asia has naturally become a focus of interest for agronomists at home and abroad. Some Japanese agronomists have suggested that rice in China was introduced from India and Japan, and that the species should accordingly be named the Indian type and Japanese type. Although in the 1960s, Chinese agronomists proposed a local origin of rice in China based on ancient Chinese literature, it did not receive much attention due to the lack of supporting physical evidence. The discovery of the Hemudu rice crop proved the theory of the local origin for the first time, and the scientific name of "Asian cultivated rice", determined by China, was recognized by the world. Its Indian and Japanese subspecies were named as "indica" and "japonica" respectively. This discovery fundamentally disproved the Indian origin of rice farming (稻作农业印度起源说) or the Assam-Yunnan origin of rice farming (印度阿萨姆—中国云南地区起源说), and established the scientific basis for the theory that rice farming originated in the middle and lower reaches of the Yangtze River.

After the discovery of the Hemudu culture, the Japanese archeological and agronomic circle turned to the idea that the Japanese rice crop originated in China, a fact well established in Chinese academia. Professor Takayasu Higuchi (樋口隆康), a renowned Japanese archeologist, summed up "three rice routes" into Japan respectively[1]: from North China, Central China, and South China. The "Central China Route", also known as the "Middle Route", refers to the direct spread of rice from the mouth of the Yangtze River eastward to Kyushu, and also to the south of the Korean Peninsula at the same time; it is also said to have first reached the south of the Korean Peninsula before reaching Kyushu. This rice route has attracted the attention of Chinese and Japanese scholars, due to abundant prehistoric rice remains in the lower reaches of the Yangtze River, mainly in Hemudu, and the discovery of the large-scale settlement site of Yoshinogari in Saga, Japan.

In September 1983, Professor An Zhimin (安志敏), a famous archeologist in China, attended the 31st session of the International Congress of Human Sciences in Asia and North Africa in Kyoto, Japan, and introduced the important discoveries of the Hemudu culture to scholars from various countries in a paper titled "On the Hemudu Culture". He said, "Several Neolithic culture elements of the Hemudu culture and its successors may also have influenced prehistoric Japan. For example, the jade, lacquerware, and a rudiment of rice farming in the Jōmon Period, as well as stilt houses in the Yayoi Period and later periods, can all be traced back to origins in the lower reaches of the Yangtze River. The discovery of wooden oars and pottery boat models at the Hemudu Site and the distribution of similar sites in the Zhoushan Islands along the coast can at least prove Hemudu people's ability to navigate the sea. Especially, when the penannular jade pieces,

---

[1] 樋口隆康. 国際東洋学会議の成果—稲作は直接中国から，安志敏氏が渡来経路で新学説— [N]. 読売新聞夕刊　1983-09-16(3).

lacquerware, and rudimentary rice farming in the Jōmon Period are taken into consideration, prehistoric Japan seems to have been linked to the Neolithic culture of the lower reaches of the Yangtze River fairly closely."[1] This led to the speculation in the Japanese archeological community that rice farming may have been directly introduced into Japan by sea. In some newspapers, reports were published that the exchange between Japan and China could be dated back to as far as 5,000 BC.

In 1989, at the Saga Forum for Japan-China Friendship, Professor An Zhimin made a comprehensive review on rice farming, wood farming tools, stilt houses, penannular earrings (jade and stone pieces), lacquerware, wood clogs, li-shaped (鬲形的) pottery, stamped pottery, sea currents and transportation. His article "Yoshinogari and the Chinese Jiangnan Culture"[2] introduces the Site of the Moated Yoshinogari Settlement in Japan, and elaborates on the relationship between the Yayoi culture (弥生文化) represented by Yoshinogari (3rd century BC to 3rd century AD) and the Chinese Jiangnan culture, from the perspective of the origin of moated settlements, the stilt houses with long ridges and short eaves, rice farming, wooden farming tools, wooden clogs, metalware, mound tombs, and urn burials.[3]

In his book *Yunnan—The Origin of the Japanese*[4] (《 倭族之源——云南 》), Kenzaburo Torigoe (鸟越宪三郎) states that the Wa people had their ancestors in Yunnan, China, who later migrated outwards through various rivers, mainly the Yangtze River. According to the excavation of the remains of rice and stilt houses in Hemudu, he also claims that their Yunnan ancestors migrated to Hemudu in the lower reaches of the Yangtze River about 7,000 years ago, then went north from Hemudu to Shandong Peninsula and finally crossed the sea to Japan, becoming the Wa people as

---

① 安志敏. 长江下游史前文化对海东的影响 [J]. 考古，1984 (5)：439-448
② 安志敏. 日本吉野里和中国江南文化 [J]. 东南文化，1990 (5)：191-199.
③ 安志敏. 日本吉野里和中国江南文化 [J]. 东南文化，1990 (5)：191-199.
④ 鸟越宪三郎. 倭族之源——云南 [M]. 昆明：云南人民出版社，1985.

they were called in history literature. So, he identifies the Hemudu ancients as the ancestors of the modern Japanese. As a result, Japan set up a special research association for the historic study of cultural exchange in East Asia, and sent academic investigation groups, including the famous scholars like Takayasu Higuchi, Tadayo Watanabe, Mitsuji Fukunaga, Daisuke Naito, Fuminori Sugaya, Kazumi Shirakihara, and Kansuke Kim (金关恕), to the lower reaches of the Yangtze River to conduct scientific investigation in the years after 1989, with Hemudu as the focus of their investigation. As various Japanese non-governmental associations made pilgrimages to Hemudu, there was an interesting incident. In the early 1990s, a Japanese scholar visited the Hemudu Site so many times within six months that it aroused a high degree of vigilance from the local public security department and the museum staff on duty were asked to have an eye on him. Of course it turned out to be a false alarm, but it proved the high status of the Hemudu culture in the minds of the Japanese people at the time.

3. The Starting Point of the Study on the Culture of the Austronesian Culture (南岛语族文化)

The ethnographic term "Austronesians", or "South Islanders", or "Malayo-Polynesians", refers to a group of indigenous peoples with ethnolinguistic affinities and similar cultural connotations, living on the Pacific islands, ranging from Taiwan of China in the north, through Southeast Asia in the middle, finally to the three major islands in the southwest Pacific, and from Easter Island (复活节岛) in the east to Madagascar in the west. The Austronesians are namely the Malays (马来人), Micronesians (密克罗尼西亚人), Melanesians (美拉尼西亚人), and Polynesians (波利尼西亚人), with a total population of over 200 million, forming a very heterogeneous ethnocultural system.

The academic communities in China and abroad have been exploring their origins for a long time. In the early 20th century, scholars of history and archeology in China explored the cultural origins of Austronesians mainly within the academic framework of Chinese ethnohistory, and connected them in varying degrees to the ancient Baiyue culture (百越文化[①]) in China. In an interview, Australian scholar Peter Bellwood (彼得·贝尔伍德) said that he regards Hemudu as the origin of the cultural phenomenon that covered the whole area of South Asia and the South Pacific islands. And an increasing number of experts agree that a branch of the Malayo-Polynesian originated in the coastal areas of Southeast China.[②]

In the 1930s, Robert von Heine-Geldern (罗伯特·海尼–格尔顿), a German archeologist, pointed out that stepped adzes distributed in the Pacific Rim were first introduced from the southeastern coast of China to the Philippines, and then to Polynesia.[③] Lin Huixiang (林惠祥) also noted the relationship between the stepped adzes in Chinese southeastern coastal areas and the Neolithic cultures of Southeast Asia and the Pacific area. He suggested that stepped adzes may have been associated with the manufacture of canoes and that stepped adzes were first produced in the southeastern provinces of China — Fujian, Guangdong, Zhejiang, Jiangxi, Jiangsu, and Anhui, and then spread northward to North China and Northeast China, and finally southeastward to the Philippines, and the Polynesian islands.[④]

Since the discovery of the Hemudu culture, many scholars have noticed that as far as the form is concerned, stepped adzes have an obvious relation with the arc-backed stone adzes with an asymmetrical edge found at the Hemudu Site. In Zhejiang, there is a very clear tadze evolution from the Hemudu form to the Liangzhu form or later forms, and the development sequence is complete. So scholars agree that adzes originated in the Hemudu

---

① "Baiyue" used to be the term referring to the descents of the Yue Kingdom, a vassal state of the Spring and Autumn Period, who later moved to the coastal provinces in Southern China, like Zhejiang, Fujian, Guangdong, Hainan, Guangxi, and even Northern Vietnam.

② 贝尔伍德，洪晓纯. 彼德·贝尔伍德 (Peter Bellwood) 教授访谈录 [J]. 南方文物，2011 (3)：22-29.

③ Heine-Geldern, R. von. Urheimat und früheste Wanderungen der Austronesier[J]. *Anthropos*, 1932(27): 543-619.

④ 石奕龙，孟令国. 林惠祥先生的有段石锛研究及其启迪 [J]. 湖北民族学院学报（哲学社会科学版），2019 (3)：104-110.

culture.

There were two routes for the spread of the Hemudu culture to the outside world: the land route and the sea route.[①] The sea route relied on people's aviation ability. Two groups of evidence have been recognized. Firstly, the wooden oars were the most common wooden production tool of the Hemudu culture, and more than 20 pieces have been found so far. Although no actual canoes have been found to date, canoes have been found at the Kuahuqiao Site（跨湖桥遗址）in Xiaoshan District, Hangzhou City, which predated the Hemudu culture by a thousand years. It is generally believed that there must be a boat if there is a paddle, so researchers think it is only a matter of time before the discovery of boats in the Hemudu culture. Secondly, a large number of fish skeletons, mussel shells, water chestnuts, and Gorgon fruit were unearthed in the Hemudu culture, which proved aquatic plants and animals were an important food source. Of particular importance were the remains of marine animals living in deep water such as whales, sharks, and tunas, in addition to the remains of marine fishes living in river mouths like flathead grey mullet and the *Gymnocranius*. For the catch of deep water fishes, the seafaring vessel was a must. Furthermore, the fact that some Hemudu ancients already crossed the sea and moved to the Zhoushan Islands about 6,000 years ago indicates that they already had had primitive means of navigation and had mastered the technique of sailing in the offshore areas. The canoes excavated in the Kuahuqiao Site were lighter and more suitable for navigation on inland lakes and rivers. But if wooden frames had been tied to one side or both sides of them, they would become single-outrigger or double-outrigger boats, and their ability to withstand wind and waves would be greatly enhanced. This is evidenced by the fact that such outrigger boats are still used by some of the modern Austronesians. Therefore, there are elements of maritime culture in the Hemudu culture, and the Hemudu people, as one of the first peoples to sail on the sea and live on coastal islands might

---

① 王海明，刘淑华. 河姆渡文化的扩散与传播 [J]. 南方文物，2005（3）：114-118，113.

have been an important origin of the Austronesians.

4. Contributions to the Chinese Civilization

The Hemudu culture made great contributions to the development of the Chinese civilization in the following aspects. Firstly, the Hemudu ancients invented the mortise-and-tenon joints during the construction of stilt houses. As they lived in low-lying places surrounded by lakes, marshes, and hills, the stilt houses were a necessary invention to adapt to the rainy and humid living environment, and they also functioned effectively in defending against wild animals. Since then, the stilt house has been popular in the minority areas of southern China and on the islands off the Pacific coast, which shows its far-reaching influence. Moreover, the more than one hundred pieces of mortise and tenon woodwork excavated in the building remains are particularly striking, including column head tenons, column foot tenons, beam head tenons, tenons with dowel holes, middle column mortises, corner column mortises, latticed railing mortises, and rabbet joints. The tenons and mortises used on the various beams and pillars were large enough to withstand the forces of tension and pressure, making the structure a marvel of architectural science. In particular, the length-to-width ratio of the cross-section is 4 : 1, which has been called the "empirical cross-section" later. Experts on ancient architecture were amazed at the discovery of large numbers of timber components joined by mortises and tenons. The discovery proved that this skill was already deftly employed by the Hemudu people about 7,000 years ago. And it has pushed the history of the technique of mortise-and-tenon wood construction in China back by more than 3,000 years.

Secondly, the Hemudu people invented wells. A total of 3 wells were found at the Hemudu Site. One used to be a shallow pot-shaped puddle, 1.35-meter deep, with 28 wood piles remaining on the outside to form a circular fence with a diameter of 6 meters, and a square shaft in the center with a side length of about 2 meters. The four walls of the shaft were surrounded by dense timber piles, and on the inside, four thick round or half-round timbers were connected with tenon and mortise, forming a square frame to support the four walls. On the top, 16 long round timbers formed a square frame to reinforce the shaft opening and the walls. Judging from the fence around the periphery, the radiating structure of long thin logs, and the fragments of reed mats, the well might have been covered with a simple well pavilion. This is by far the earliest wood-structured well in China. The Hemudu wells were also linked with the origin of the character " 井 ". "The two forms and of this character correspond to the structure of Hemudu wells with frames made of logs and Liangzhu wells with frames made of curved wooden boards."[1]

Thirdly, the Hemudu people were already able to weave. Relics related to weaving were found in the Hemudu culture. China was the first country to produce silk fabric. Although no silk textiles have been found in the Hemudu culture, the image of the silkworm has already been discovered. Two cap-shaped ivory vessels with the image of silkworms on the outer wall were unearthed at the Hemudu Site. One was carved with 2 bands of string pattern interspersed with a diagonal woven pattern, with a band of silkworm pattern at a lower place; the other was carved with a broad band of diagonal woven pattern and a band of silkworm-like pattern (incomplete), Although the image of the silkworm is not sufficient to prove that silk weaving had already been in existence, many artifacts related to weaving and knitting have been found in the Hemudu culture, such as thick and thin ropes, reed mats, and bone daggers（古匕） with woven patterns. Many more production tools for sewing and weaving have been found, including bone needles（骨针） and spindle whorls, and important loom parts such as warp setting bars, weft beaters, shuttles, and cloth beams. Most importantly, at the Tianluoshan Site, the discovery of 2 balls of fine thread proved the ancients' rudimentary weaving craft.

Fourthly, the Hemudu people were one of the first peoples to invent and use lacquerware in China. The excavated Hemudu wooden bowls were

---

① 谈大庆. 浅谈井字的起源与发展 [J]. 古文字，2002（1）：61-62.

coated with a shiny vermilion pigment. Mr. Li Peiji (李培基) from the Institute of Polymer Research of the Chinese Academy of Sciences took the sample of the coating and identified it as organic lacquer. There are many other lacquer objects from the Hemudu culture, such as wooden cylinders, bird-shaped (butterfly-shaped) wooden objects, and lacquer-painted pottery pieces. One of the wooden cylinders still retains a shiny black lacquer exterior with a golden hue. The discovery of these lacquer objects has pushed the history of Chinese lacquer craft from the Shang Dynasty [as evidenced by lacquer found at the Taixi Site (台西遗址) of Gaocheng District in Hebei Province] to about 7,000 years ago.

Finally, the discovery of the Hemudu culture has raised a new question in ethnology. Physical anthropologists have reconstructed the image of the Hemudu people from the human skeleton unearthed. They were of medium stature, 1.63–1.69 meters tall, and exhibited the following characteristics: broad zygomatic bones, accentuated zygomatic arches, a relatively rounded orbital margin, a broad and flat nasal root, and shovel-shaped incisors. But other features like long heads and low and wide noses are more common in some species of the black race. Such ethnological features need further study.

II. The Liangzhu Culture

The subsequent culture in the area of Ningbo after the Hemudu culture was discovered in the late 1970s and early 1980s during a survey of ancient cultural sites on both sides of the Yuyao River. At the Qianxihu Site (前溪湖遗址) in Yuyao County, relics such as the fin-footed sand-tempered red pottery tripod, black-coated gray-clay bamboo-handle *dou*, and stepped stone adzes (有段石锛), were found. These relics were found in Ningbo for the first time, though a common assemblage in the Liangzhu culture on the northern shore of Hangzhou Bay. It seems that after the Hemudu culture, a successor culture equivalent to the Liangzhu culture existed in Ningbo.

Research on the subsequent culture was carried out in step with the further study on the Hemudu culture. In the late 1980s and early 1990s, sites such as Cihu, Xiaodongmen, Mingshanhou, Tashan, and Zishan were excavated, where the layers of the subsequent cultures were found directly superimposed on the third and fourth layers of the late Hemudu culture. Some extraordinary findings were made. The Cihu Site is the one where cultural layers of the subsequent culture were firstly found in the Ningbo-Shaoxing Plain (宁绍平原). And the Mingshanhou Site is the one where the super-imposition of the layers of the successor culture on the layers of the Hemudu culture is the clearest and where the cultural accumulation is the richest. Its second to seventh cultural layers are further divided into two stages: the early stage is represented by cultural layers 5 and H14, while the late stage includes the fourth and the subsequent layers. Beneath the seventh cultural layer is the rammed earth platform of brownish-yellow sand and yellow clay, which is the first of its kind in Ningbo.

Other subsequent sites, such as the Qianxihu Site and the Yangqi'ao Site (杨歧岙遗址) in Yuyao County, feature only the Hemudu culture. But the two were only investigated, without formal excavation. In 1994 and 1997, the excavation of the Shaxi Site (沙溪遗址) was carried out in Chaiqiao Town (柴桥镇), Beilun District, Ningbo City, covering an area of 370 square meters. Some of the unearthed artifacts displayed elements inherited from the Hemudu culture, but the majority of them were surprisingly similar to those of the Liangzhu culture on the north shore of Hangzhou Bay. Meanwhile, other artifacts show local marine culture characteristics.

Given their link and distinction to the typical Liangzhu culture, archeologists gave these subsequent cultures two names, "the south type of the Liangzhu culture" for its distribution area along the south bank of the Qiantang River, and "the Mingshanhou type of the Liangzhu culture" (良渚文化名山后类型), which was named after its most representative and typical site. But the two names refer to the same culture. To this point, a relatively clear sequence of prehistoric cultural development in Ningbo has been established, including the four phases of the Hemudu culture and the south type of the Liangzhu culture (or the Mingshanhou type of the Liangzhu culture).

The type of the Liangzhu culture in Ningbo after the Hemudu culture was poorly preserved, and the excavated areas were so limited that we cannot have a comprehensive understanding of its village form. Generally speaking, the villages were small in size and inhabited for a relatively short period of time, leaving relatively thin cultural layers. Houses, generally ground buildings, were built on the slopes of hillsides to facilitate drainage. The construction procedures were as follows: first, a foundation trench was dug and filled with stone and soil; then, earthen walls were built and covered with rafters; finally, a roof was added on top. There were also stilt houses, as pits of various sizes and depths for the pillars were found, some filled with red burned clay and some with rocks at the bottom. A rammed square platform (人工夯筑土台), which was a ritual building for sacrifice, was also found.

Only a few small tombs were found scattered around the houses, generally shallow, rectangular shaft tombs with several pottery objects buried in them.

Clan burials and big tombs in rammed earth platforms with large numbers of jade burial objects, common in the Liangzhu culture on the north shore of Hangzhou Bay, were not found in Ningbo.

Unlike sites on the tableland in the Hangzhou-Jiaxing-Huzhou Plain, the sites in Ningbo were all located in piedmont areas near rivers or lakes. This provided the natural conditions to engage in both rice farming and dry land farming. And the adjacency to mountains and waters also facilitated fishing, hunting, and gathering. The widespread rice cultivation can be proved by the prevalent rice hull marks on the walls of pottery ware. But the status of other crops is less clear, as no evidence has been found. Since what the Liangzhu ancients on the northern shore of Hangzhou Bay grew included sesame, peanuts, gourds and melons, it might have been the same for people in Ningbo. The newly found production tools like stone plows, stone plowshares, and stone hoes (石耨) marked the agricultural development of the Liangzhu culture here. The stone plow could turn soil continuously, greatly improving the efficiency of land tilling and promoting the development of rice farming. The stone plowshare could be used to break up large pieces of soil dug out with the plow, level the field, and turn the soil in dry land. The stone hoe was used to weed. Stone knives came in a variety of shapes and sizes, with different functions. Long and half-moon-shaped knives were used for harvesting rice ears, while the rest were probably kitchen knives used for cutting animal meat and various vegetables and fruits. The variety of livestock surpassed that of the Hemudu culture. It has been confirmed that pigs, sheep, dogs, and cattle were already domesticated. But fishing, hunting, and gathering were still important and indispensable sources of food at the time. Since many of the sites were already comparatively far from mountains and close to rivers and lakes, fishing and collecting water chestnuts must have been more important than picking wild fruits and hunting in the mountains. There were a large number of stone arrowheads (石镞) unearthed, but very few bone and wood arrowheads. The reason may lie in the fact that stone arrowheads, with a much sharper edge, brought about a greater harvest.

Handicraft was already separated from agriculture, and non-agricultural laborers who were specialized in the production of pottery and jade emerged. Pottery was still the main household utensil, generally made on the pottery wheel, with a wide variety of shapes, such as tripods, *dou*, pots, jars, ring-footed plates, ring-footed pots, *gui* (簋，food container with two side ears), bowls, and cups. A few pottery pieces were stamped with cord patterns, and most were decorated with string patterns, poked points, or openwork patterns in this period. The most advanced pottery craft was the clay pottery with black coating. After careful surface polish, pottery vessels were put into the reducing environment of a well-sealed kiln for the infiltration of charcoal to form the black coating, then carved with bird motifs, or motifs with a bird head and a snake body. The mysterious motifs were so cleverly and skillfully composed with smooth lines that it is assumed that they must have been carved by professional craftsmen. The time-consuming and finely carved black coating pottery may have evolved from a utilitarian vessel into a ritual vessel for a specific purpose. Another handicraft invention was wood clogs. The clogs, once popular all over the country, were introduced to Japan, and southeast Asian countries long ago, where they continued to be used for a considerable period of time. In southern China, clogs were still worn by farmers in summer in modern times. In Japan, clogs, and kimono, as a symbol of the Yamato or traditional Japan, are still worn today. So to speak, the invention of clogs by the prehistoric people of Ningbo was an important contribution to the world's ancient civilizations.

Production tools like axes, adzes, arrowheads, spindle whorls, knives, scythes, plows, plowshares, and hoes were mainly made of stone, all of them finely crafted, varied in shape, and widely used. There were many large and heavy ceramic mortars, which were undoubtedly a major improvement in food processing, as they could be used to process tubers and cereals with more efficiency. Paddles, drills, adze handles made of wood were also found. Tools such as bone chisels, bone needles, and bone awls (骨锥) were still found to be in use, but the variety and number were significantly fewer than in the Hemudu culture.

No jade ritual objects like *cong* (琮，jade), *bi* (璧，disk), and *yue* (钺，battle-axe) have been found in Ningbo to date, with the exception of small human body ornaments such as *jue, huang*, jade tubes, and jade cones. This is the most important difference from the Liangzhu culture on the north shore of Hangzhou Bay.

The distribution of the Liangzhu culture in Ningbo was still concentrated on the sides of the Yuyao River, mostly overlapping with the layers of the Hemudu culture. At several excavated sites, the layers of the Liangzhu culture were directly superimposed on the third and fourth phases of the Hemudu culture. But at other sites, merely cultural deposits of the Liangzhu culture were found. It proved that sites of the Liangzhu culture were more extensively and densely distributed than those of the Hemudu culture, and that many places that had been unsuitable for human habitation were populated in this period.

Judging from the superimposed cultural layers and the characteristics of artifacts excavated at the Mingshanhou Site, we can roughly classify the Liangzhu culture in Ningbo-Shaoxing Plain into two phases.

The early phase is represented by culture layers 5 and H14 at the Mingshanhou Site, and the upper layers at the Cihu Site. The earliest can date back to around 5,300 years ago.

The late phase is represented by the fourth and subsequent layers at the Mingshanhou Site, the fifth and sixth layers at the Tashan Site in Xiangshan County, and the Yangqi'ao Site in Yuyao County. The radioactive dating for this phase is still in lack.

The Liangzhu culture on the northern shore of Hangzhou Bay dating back to 5,300 to 4,000 years ago, has been divided into three or five phases by researchers of different opinions. The Liangzhu culture in Ningbo may roughly be the same.

So far, the cultural deposits of the excavated sites vary in thickness and richness, but the relics have been basically similar in terms of type, shape, and decorative style. The series of pottery were composed mainly of sand-tempered red pottery, gray-clay pottery, and clay pottery with a black coating. Utensils such as fin-legged tripods, T-legged tripods, bamboo handle *dou*, jars of various forms, and double-lugged jars were most common. Though the conical red clay pottery jars with prick designs and sand-tempered pottery jars were found in small numbers, they could be seen at almost every site. The common stone tools were triangular perforated stone plows, stone hoes, stone plowshares, stone scythes, stepped stone adzes, willow-leaf-shaped stone arrowheads, and perforated stone axes. The quality, types, shapes, and decorations of pottery were dramatically different from those in the Hemudu culture, and featured a large proportion of charcoal-mixed pottery and a distinctive form of *fu* with stamped cord patterns. There were also differences in the production methods and shapes of stone tools. Only a few heritages of the Hemudu culture survived. But these cultural sites showed a high degree of consistency with the Liangzhu culture on the northern shore of Hangzhou Bay, in terms of the quality and colors of pottery, the varieties, decoration methods, and shapes of pottery and stone tools, as well as the construction of earthen platforms, with exceptions in only several artifacts. Therefore, the two cultures on both shores of Hangzhou Bay can be classified as the same one. Their differences in cultural connotations may have resulted from their geographical distribution and different time of existence.

III. Archeology of the Shang and Zhou Dynasties

After the Liangzhu culture, the central plains were ruled by the dynasties named Xia, Shang and Zhou successively. Meanwhile, Ningbo, close to Shaoxing, the Yue capital, was a territory of the Yue Tribe. So there was great social and economic development and population growth. Primitive villages were densely distributed in Ningbo, but their cultural layers were severely damaged by later activities because of their shallow burial. In 1978, the trial excavation of the Qian'ao Site (钱盉遗址) was carried out in Hengxi Town (横溪镇), Yinzhou District, Ningbo City, covering an area of 48 square meters. The cultural deposits were divided into three layers. In addition to the discovery of a small number of wooden building remains, a lot of Shang and Zhou pottery ware were unearthed, including clay pottery, stamped hard pottery, and proto-porcelain. Relics of copper, stone, and jade were found, as well as carbonized rice, leaves, and fruits. Their dating corresponded to the dynasties established on the central plains, namely the late Shang Dynasty, Western Zhou Dynasty, the Spring and Autumn Period, and the Warring States Period. At the previously mentioned sites, such as Xiangjiashan, Tashan, and Xiaodongmen, relics and ash pits of Shang and Zhou were found as well.

Yue people's earthen mound tombs and mound tombs with stone rooms dominated the archeological findings of the Shang and Zhou Dynasties in Ningbo. They were found in large numbers and quite well preserved. But they did not attract the attention of archeologists until 1980, when the stone-chambered mound tombs in the Huangpo Hill (黄婆山 , formally known as 航坞山 , Hangwu Hill) of Qiaotou Town (桥头镇), Cixi County, were sorted out. In 1984, rescue excavations were carried out in tombs at Pengdong Town (彭东乡) and Dong'an Town (东安乡), Cixi County.

Their datings corresponded to the Western Zhou Dynasty, the Spring and Autumn Period, and the Warring States Period on the central plains. This is a preliminary exploration of earthen mound tombs and mound tombs with stone rooms in Ningbo, and provides new materials for the research on the distribution patterns and cultural landscape of these remains.

In 1992, the excavation of Pier 1 at the Laohushan Site (老虎山遗址) in Mingwei Village (明伟村), Yuyao County reflected the changes in the burial system in the Ningbo-Shaoxing area during the Warring States Period. The burial objects showed cultural characteristics of the vassal kingdom of Chu (楚国), as a result of the conquering of Yue by Chu at the end of the Spring and Autumn Period and the influence of the Chu culture on the Yue culture.

Since 2007, a number of archeological surveys, explorations, and trial excavations have been carried out in the vicinity of Wangjiaba Village (王家坝村), in the north of Chengshan Ferry (城山渡), Cicheng Town, covering an area of nearly 500,000 square meters. In a trial excavation area of about 50 square meters, some collapsed buildings associated with the urban facilities of the ancient Gouzhang City[①] were found, as well as the building foundations of stepped wooden buildings and wooden stilt buildings, a sloping cobblestone road. Outside the city, there were kiln sites and burial areas. The excavations also yielded hundreds of specimens with a long time range from the Spring and Autumn Period, the Warring States Period, to the Western Jin Dynasty and the Eastern Jin Dynasty, including a number of building parts such as imbrexes (筒瓦), plate tiles, eave tiles (瓦当), and bricks, as well as daily utensils of stamped pottery, clay pottery, proto-porcelain, celadon, and lacquered wood. The discovery of the ancient city of Gouzhang is a major breakthrough in the archeology of the Shang and Zhou Dynasties in Ningbo in the 21st century.

Ningbo was the territory of the vassal state Yue during the Shang and

---

① Gouzhang, located in what is nowadays Cixi County, Ningbo, was an ancient city established in the fifth century BC by King Goujian of Yue.

Zhou Dynasties. The Yue tribe created a glorious culture and established a powerful kingdom, which finally destroyed the state of Wu and dominated the Yangtze River Region and the Huaihe River Region (淮河流域). Gouzhang City, the earliest city in the area of today's Ningbo, was well developed both socially and economically, as a result of its adjacency to the Yue capital. The city was roughly rectangular in shape, 470 meters in length, 120–200 meters in width, and 1,200 meters in circumference, with a total area of about 100,000 square meters. Stepped wooden buildings, stilt style wooden buildings and pebble-paved streets have been excavated in the city. Functional blocks were well established, with government offices, living and commercial areas located in the city, and burial sites, kilns and docks outside the city. An important sea port for the state Yue, it was built by King Goujian (勾践) to serve both military and commercial purposes. In the city, shipbuilding workshops were set up, naval forces trained, and traders from overseas assembled.

Gouzhang was but a small border city with a population of a few thousands then. However, its existence was significant for Ningbo in two aspects: for one thing, it was the first city in its history; for another, it was essential in promoting the economic development of the region, particularly for the plain in the east of Ningbo. During the Shang and Zhou Dynasties, the villages were more densely populated than ever before. Fragments of stamped hard pottery and proto-porcelain from the settlement of that time can be found almost everywhere in the hilly terrains or at the confluence of streams and rivers. However, as no ideal settlement site has been located for archeological excavation so far, not much is known about those villages. Probably they maintained the previous stilt houses and ground houses. Earthen mound tombs and mound tombs with stone rooms, the distinctive burial forms for the Yue people, were found in large numbers on the ridges, hillsides, and sloping areas of the coastal hills. The tombs were built with sand and earth into the shape of a mound. But their sizes were many times larger than ordinary tombs, ranging from two to three hundred square meters to thousands of square meters. When some mounds were dug up, stone rooms were found with a passage in the front; in others, there were flat planes known as "stone beds" built with small stones, though in the more elaborate ones four stone walls, commonly known as a "stone frame", were built; in still others, no construction of stone was found. In the well-preserved tombs, there were piles of burial objects, one group at least, or as many as five or six groups, and ten groups at most, mainly composed of proto-celadon and stamped hard pottery. The archeological term for mounds without enclosed stone rooms is earthen mound tombs, while those with enclosed stone rooms and passages are called mound tombs with stone rooms.

The process of tomb building was as follows. First, a large flat area was leveled out on a ridge or hilltop, then a rectangular earth platform was built in the middle, on which the burial goods and coffin were placed, and finally, earth was piled up into a mound around the platform. From about the early Western Zhou Dynasty, cobblestones or other small stones were laid on the platform to form a "stone bed", and for more sophisticated occasions walls were built on all sides to form a "stone frame". On this basis, around the middle Western Zhou Dynasty, the ceiling and floor of the tomb and its surrounding walls were all built with stones, forming an airtight "stone room", and the front passage was also built with stones. A mound was generally composed of multiple tombs, with the later tombs built on a slightly flattened slope of the sealed mound or in a shallow pit dug into the mound before being covered with more earth and turned into a new mound. Some mound tombs were merely built on top of the existing mound. As a result, the number of burials continued to increase, and the mound grew in both height and size. The mound tombs with stone rooms commonly has one tomb, with a few exceptions of containing two or three tombs, where the entry, the "sealing stone", could be conveniently dismantled and then re-installed. This accounts for why several groups of artifacts from different times could be seen placed together in the stone chambers, and signs of re-burial of the deceased by later generations could also be recognized from the traces of resealing the rooms.

During the Shang and Zhou Dynasties, rice continued to be the main food crop of the people in Ningbo. Rice farming was more advanced than before, as evidenced by the improvement of farming tools and the widespread use of bronze tools. Traditional tools such as stone plows, stone scythes, and stone knives were still in use, but more finely crafted and used in a larger area than before. As bronze was expensive, on the central plains, bronze wares were mostly used for ceremonial purposes. However, most of the bronze objects in Ningbo were tools for agricultural production, including hoes, shovels, sharpeners, harrows, plows, axes, knives, and sickles. The greater variety and a more refined and specialized division of these tools tremendously promoted rice farming.

Pottery, shipbuilding, and textiles became the main crafts of the time.

As household utensils made of stamped hard pottery were popular during the Shang and Zhou Dynasties, their fragments have often been found in settlement sites. They were stamped with a wide range of decorations, including trellis pattern (方格纹), latticework (窗格纹), rhombus pattern (菱形纹), linen pattern (麻布纹), mi-character (米字) pattern, and rectangular spiral pattern (回纹). Its firing temperature was 1,050℃ , much higher than the 900℃ temperature for ordinary clay pottery or sand-tempered pottery. As a result, stamped hard pottery has an increased mechanical strength. However, the disadvantage was that the hardness of this clay limited its plasticity. It was difficult to apply the advanced fast wheel technique in its production. So, clay had to be kneaded into shape by hand, or made into clay bars, and then coiled into a rough form. Therefore, stamped hard pottery was coarse in texture, and most ware were large storage vessels like jars and jugs.

After thousands of years of searching and experimentation, the material "porcelain clay" was discovered. Its advantages were worth noting. The plastic porcelain clay could be molded on a fast pottery wheel and endure high temperatures. As a result, the clayware had both regular shapes and high mechanical strength after firing. After the glaze was applied to the surface, the clayware was fired at a temperature of about 1,200 ℃. The product was proto-porcelain, smooth and shiny, with a low water absorption rate, which was a major leap forward in history following the invention of stamped hard pottery. Proto-porcelain was mainly excavated in tombs, and less often in residential sites. There were many types: tripods for food cooking, containers for water or wine like jars, pots, bowls, plates, and basins, and containers for food like *dou*, and *gui*. The colors of proto-porcelain were greenish brown, brown, sauce brown, or black brown. Although the glaze was not evenly applied, the vitrification effect was quite good.

Shipbuilding was an important craft of people in Gouzhang, an important port of the Yue Kingdom. As we have already mentioned, more than 7,000 years ago the Hemudu people already mastered the craft of making canoes and bamboo-rafts（竹木筏）and started sailing in offshore waters. Ningbo people's shipbuilding techniques were greatly improved during the Shang and Zhou Dynasties. A bronze *yue* of the Zhou Dynasty discovered in Yinzhou District featured a picture of 4 Yue people with feather crowns rowing a boat, which fully illustrated that boats played an important role in their life. From ancient documents, the Yue people were already able to build small boats, light boats, war boats, bronze ships, and ships with an upper deck, some of which were so large that they were "more than ten feet high". To build such a large ship naturally required a special shipbuilding workshop and a government office dedicated to shipbuilding, called the "boat hall" （舟室）or "boat palace"（船宫）. The Yue people made ships not only for their own use, but also for the royal family of the Zhou Dynasty and other vassal kingdoms. There was an exact transaction record of 300 ships at one delivery.

Textile production was also an important handicraft. At sites like Qian'ao, Xiaodongmen, and Tashan, weaving tools such as stone spindle whorls, pottery spindle whorls, and needles from the Shang and Zhou Dynasties were found. Although no textile materials of this period was found, the flourishing of textile production was recorded in the *Yuejue Shu* (*Glory of the Yue*, 《越

绝书 》) and *Wu-Yue Chunqiu* (*Annals of Wu and Yue*, 《 吴越春秋 》)[1]. Story had it that when the Yue Kingdom succumbed to the Wu Kingdom as the result of its military failure, the King of Yue (越王) motivated his people to produce 100,000 pieces of cloth from wild ko-hemp collected from the mountains to please the King of Wu (吴王). The quality of these fabrics was excellent. As a song goes, "It is lighter than silk." These historic writings prove that the Yue people were good at weaving. As part of the Yue Kingdom, Ningbo must also have been a place with well-developed textile production.

Generally speaking, the prehistory of Ningbo can be traced back to only about 7,000 years ago, and beyond that it was almost blank. The prehistoric culture of Ningbo existed later than cultures of other regions, but it played an important role in China's ancient civilizations and was recorded in history as a representative of the ancient civilization of the Yangtze River Region, renowned both at home and abroad. The major achievements about 7,000 years ago — the well-developed rice farming and the farming tool *si*, the stilt houses with superb mortise and tenon construction, the wooden wells, the lacquer painting techniques, and the unique charcoal-tempered black pottery — were all known across the world. Among these, the invention and spread of stilt houses, lacquerware, stepped stone adzes and two-hole stone knives not only influenced other primitive cultures in the surrounding areas, but also had a profound impact on the primitive cultures of Southeast Asian countries and Japan. The stepped adzes spread to the Pacific islands and became the starting point of the study on the Austronesians. The development of the culture in Ningbo went through several stages. Around 5,300 years ago, the culture in Ningbo was integrated into the Liangzhu culture through the cultural exchanges of the locals with other peoples in the vicinity, which turned a new leaf in Chinese civilization. During the Shang and Zhou Dynasties, Ningbo was part of the Yue Kingdom, which

---

[1] Yue and Wu were both vassal kingdoms of the Zhou Dynasty.

defeated the powerful adjacent Wu Kingdom and dominated the Yangtze River Region and the Huaihe River Region. During the Spring and Autumn Period and the Warring States Period, the construction of the ancient city of Gouzhang further accelerated the development of the coastal plain in the east of Ningbo, laying a solid foundation for its economy, urbanization, and function in the Maritime Silk Road. From that, it followed logically that Ningbo people made well-known achievements represented by advanced maritime transport, traditional wooden architecture with the Baoguo Temple as an typical example, and the famous Yue Kiln Celadon. All of these splendid achievements were rooted in the rich accumulation and heritage of its advanced prehistoric culture.

The Dawn in the East

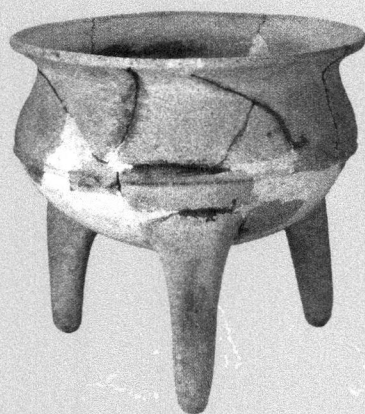

I. Environmental Changes

As the old saying goes, "The mountains feed people in the mountains, and the waters feed people by the waters." People in different regions have different lifestyles, ways of thinking, and histories, for their behavior and cultural characteristics are molded by different natural surroundings and by different geographical and climatic conditions. Such was also the case with the ancients in Ningbo, especially when they were restricted by the low levels of productivity during the prehistoric period.

The area of Ningbo is a vast coastal plain bounded by the Tiantai Mountains and the Siming Mountains in the southwest. The crisscross rivers and water networks, the fertile land, and a warm climate made it an ideal place for the settlement of primitive people. However, Ningbo had gone through many major geological and climate changes before.

The prehistoric sites already discovered were all located in the low-lying coastal plain in the east and north of Ningbo, most of them only 2–3 meters above sea level. The short distance to the sea made the plain vulnerable to sea rises, which caused a lot of changes in the geological landscapes. Globally, there were three major marine transgressions since the late Pleistocene: the Asterorotalia, the Pseudorotalia, and the Ammonia. The last one, in particular, played a decisive role in the formation of the modern landscape of the plain of Ningbo. Around 12,000 years ago, the coastline lay at a place more than 100 meters below the current sea level, at the edge of the continental shelf and to the east of Zhoushan Islands. So to speak, the sea around Zhoushan Islands was then still land, which is evidenced by the fact that fishers have often recovered ancient animal bones from the shallow waters there in recent years. When the marine transgression began, seawater rose and gradually submerged the low-lying coastal plain and penetrated deep into the interior. It reached the highest place around 8,000 years ago, closed on the Siming Mountains and the Tiantai Mountains, submerged the whole Ningbo Plain in a shallow sea, and turned smaller hills into islands. Then, the sea level began to fall about 7,400 years ago. There were several rises and falls of the sea level later, but only modest ones. The marine sediments deposited during the marine transgression formed layers of silt 10 to 50 meters thick, and eventually resulted in the modern geomorphological pattern of the Ningbo-Shaoxing Plain. The Yuyao-Cicheng Plain, between the Siming Mountains and the Cinan Hills, was the earliest area to become land after the sea retreated.

After the formation of the Yuyao-Cicheng Plain, the Hemudu ancients began to settle down in this mountain-encircled coastal plain. The sites of Hemudu, Zishan, Tianluoshan, Fujiashan, and Tongjia'ao were the first prehistoric habitats in Ningbo after the retreat of the sea. In their earliest cultural layers, there were remains of a large variety of foraminifera (孔虫), ostracods (介形虫), diatoms, pollen from many aquatic plants, and marine animals such as sharks, whales, tunas, and sea turtles, indicating a shorter distance between the sites and the sea than today. The high salinity level of the soil also suggested that the surrounding lakes and rivers were seriously affected by the salty tide. But the Yuyao-Cicheng Plain was basically free from sea water inundation, for the strata (地层) formed during the same period contained a large number of remains of freshwater fish, bulrushes, peat, and a great many spores and pollens of graminaceous plants. Yet the low-lying plain was and is still criss-cross with rivers and lakes, with the biggest lake still existing among Hemudu Town, Erliushi Town (二六市镇), and Zhangting Town today. Although there were several changes in the sea level after that, the continual, dense distribution of sites of the Hemudu culture, the Liangzhu culture, and the dynasties such as the Xia, Shang, and Zhou on this plain proved that sea-level changes were insignificant and that the vicinity was not greatly affected by marine transgression.

During the Hemudu people's nearly 2,000-year living activities, the area of Ningbo was characterized by a high level of underground water and a large number of lakes. But there was an alternative expansion of land area and water area. Judging from the change in the number of aquatic plants and the chronology of cultural layers, the shrinking of water area and expanding of marsh area took place about 6,000–6,700 years ago and happened again 5,000–5,500 years ago. During the intervals, the water area expanded, corresponding to the deposition of a layer of silt on the second cultural layer at the Hemudu Site and a layer of greenish-grey silt 7–14 centimeters thick on the fifth layer at the Fujiashan Site, both without signs of human activities. They indicate that the sites were flooded around 6,000 years ago.

From about 6,000 years ago, other areas of the Ningbo Plain have also been rising above seawater. Pieces of land emerged one after another, and some rivers and lakes developed into marshes. Human beings began to settle in areas that were previously unsuitable for human life. Judging from the obvious increase of settlements to over 30, population growth must have been very rapid as well. From the distribution map of the Hemudu Site, it can be seen that the Hemudu people began to go out of the Yuyao-Cicheng Plain to other plains, and even crossed the sea to settle in the Zhoushan Islands, probably reaching as far as Keqiutou (壳丘头) of Pingtan Island (平潭岛), Fujian Province in the south, and the Miaodao Islands (庙岛群岛) of the former Changdao County, Shandong Province in the north.

The archeological excavations of the Hemudu Site have revealed a large number of plant and animal remains, greatly enriched our knowledge of the plant species during the times of our ancestors, and illustrated the ecological evolution of environment in Ningbo. The findings at the Hemudu Site and the Tianluoshan Site were particularly significant. At least 61 animal species were unearthed at the Hemudu Site. After preliminary identification, the vast majority were recent species, including 2 domesticated species, namely pigs and dogs, 21 species of terrestrial animals, 21 species of aquatic animals, and 8 bird species. But 8 animal species have been extinct in Ningbo today, namely the Asian elephant (亚洲象), the Sumatran rhinoceros, the Javan rhinoceros (爪哇犀), the Père David's deer, the samber deer, the stump-tailed monkey, the big-horned muntjac and the tortises. Well-preserved plant seeds and leaves of more than 25 plant species have been excavated, namely rice (including husks, stems, and leaves), acorns, water chestnuts, Gorgon fruit, acacia seeds (槐树籽), grains of Job's tears (薏仁), jujubes, and other starchy fruits and seeds, and the leaves of the red-bark oak (*Quercus gilva*, 赤皮稠), oaks, bitter evergreen chinkapin (*Castanopsis sclerophylla*), *Ficus erecta*, *Cinnamomum subavenium*, *Litsea cubeba* (山鸡椒), *Lindera chienii*, *Chloranthus spicatus*, Chinese magnolia (*Magnolia coco*), *Phoebe sheareri*, *Diospyros hainanensis*, *Camptotheca acuminata*, polygonums (蓼), Job's tears (*Coix lacryma-jobi*), moss (苔), *Ganoderma atrum* (假灵芝), *Prunus davidiana*, *Quercus glauca*, and *Castanopsis tibetana* (钩栲). Most of them were well preserved with their original colors and shapes still discernible.

The number of animals and plants found at the Tianluoshan Site was also large. The animal species unearthed in 2004 were identified to be fishes, amphibians, reptiles, birds, and mammals, less diverse than what were found at the Hemudu Site. But the plant species at the Tianluoshan Site were more diverse than the findings at the Hemudu Site. The plant seeds belonged to 18 families and 27 genera. The building timber and woodwork material were mainly gained from 3 conifer tree species, 51 broad-leaved tree species, 4 camphor tree (江浙钩樟) species of unknown genus, and 8 tree types of unknown species and genus, which greatly enriched our knowledge of the plant species of their times. In short, during the times of the Hemudu people, the animal species included not only mussels, river snails, mud crabs, tortoises and soft-shelled turtles, various kinds of fish, birds, pigs, dogs, and buffaloes, but also stump-tailed monkeys, pangolins (穿山甲), raccoon dogs (貉), jackals (豺), black bears (黑熊), tigers, elephants and rhinoceroses. The plants were mainly divided into three types: broad-leaved deciduous trees such as *Phoebe sheareri*, *Cinnamomum subavenium*, and bitter evergreen chinkapin, shrubs such as *Prunus davidiana* and jujubes, and aquatic plants such as water chestnut and Gorgon fruit.

In addition, archeologists have analyzed the spores and pollens excavated from the sites of Hemudu, Tianluoshan, and Zishan to determine the plant species to which it belonged, and thus reconstruct the vegetation conditions and climatic characteristics. Tiny spores and pollens, able to resist strong acid and alkali with the help of a hard outer wall were still well preserved and recognizable even after millions of years.

The climate changes were also significant. According to studies on global climate change over the last 10,000 years, Ningbo was warm and humid about 7,000 years ago, in the period of Holocene Climate Optimum (HCO). The climate was similar to that in southern China today. The average annual temperature was more than 4 ℃ higher, and the average annual precipitation was 800 millimeters more than today. The subtropical evergreen broad-leaved forests predominated the Siming Mountains and the Cinan Hills. Around 6,000 years ago, the temperature dropped significantly. About 5,600 years ago, the temperature dropped to a level only slightly higher than today. As a result, warm-loving tree species such as Chinese sweet gums, mushrooms, and chinquapins decreased in number or even extincted, while the number of deciduous broad-leaved trees increased. In the following 200 years, both temperature and humidity continued to decline, and the vegetation became mixed forests of deciduous, coniferous, and evergreen broad-leaved trees, mainly sawtooth oaks, Chinese sweet gums, beeches, pines, and willows. Around 5,000–5,300 years ago, the temperature rose to a level of 1 ℃ –2 ℃ higher than today, and the vegetation turned into mixed forests of evergreen broad-leaved trees and deciduous trees.

After the retreat of the sea about 7,400 years ago, lakes and rivers turned into swamps. Consequently, the Ningbo-Shaoxing Plain witnessed an unprecedented development of grassland and forests. This process of paleogeographic evolution created a variety of ecological environments, providing suitable conditions for the breeding of animals and the growth of plants of various ecological habits, which also created a unique and favorable environment for the ancient people there in their effort to obtain various production and living resources.

II. A Marvel in the History of Architecture

Primitive people attached great importance to the choice of their residence place. The distribution patterns of many a Neolithic site show that in the Yellow River Region, people chose to settle in terraces on the riversides or in tablelands at the confluence of two rivers. But in the Yangtze River Region (mainly the lower reaches of the Yangtze River), people chose to settle on high mounds near lakes and rivers or on hill slopes near water. Generally speaking, people chose to live in high, open ground areas close to water to benefit their production and living, while at the same time avoiding disadvantages or risks to their survival and development. What were the requirements of the Hemudu ancients in choosing their residence place about 7,000 years ago?

The requirements were more or less the same as those of other prehistoric people. Firstly, they needed a backdrop of mountains. Above all, the distance to the mountains should be within only a few hundred to several thousand meters, so that it was easy to go hunting and gathering in the mountains on foot and that the transport distance was short when trees were cut down to build houses. Secondly, the residents should be facing extensive waters or a plain. Vast waters were important living resources, where they could catch fish and shrimps, pick water chestnuts and Gorgon fruit, and cultivate rice in fields reclaimed from the mudflats of the lakes, rivers, and swamps. Many areas on both sides of the Yuyao-Cicheng Plain met these conditions. However, the low-lying areas facing lakes and swamps were damp and easily flooded. So the third condition was a relatively high and dry position. Therefore, the isolated hills in the front of a mountainous area were certainly the first choice, most of which were only a few meters above sea level, with the highest being no more than 60 or 70 meters above sea level.

Without doubt, their choice of settlement was aimed at the best utilization of the natural resources around them. With the help of advanced computer technology and geographical information systems, archeologists have speculated on the scope of their activities to access various living resources based on information from the various plant and animal remains excavated from the Tianluoshan Site.

The ecological environment surrounding the Tianluoshan Site was diverse, including wetlands and shrub forests in the vicinity, and forests in distant mountain areas. This environment supplied the ancients with four main food resources: rice they grew, water chestnuts and Gorgon fruit they collected, freshwater fish and animals they caught — mainly carp, deer, and short-horned water buffalo, as well as acorns they gathered in the woods of the mountains. The activities to get the first three types of the above-mentioned food were mainly carried out on the Yuyao-Cicheng Plain, within a scope of 1–3 hours' walk. For the gathering of acorns, which still grow widely in the Cinan Hills to the north of the site today, the ancients only had to walk for 2–4 hours. This suggests that the four main food resources would have been available to the Tianluoshan ancients within a distance of 3–4 hours' walk. The evidence, 20,000 plant specimens from the site belonging to more than 50 plant species, were analyzed. Among them, rice, acorns, Gorgon fruit, and water chestnuts were the most numerous and were the main species for food for the people from the early phase through the late phase; over 10 species of fruits and seeds were very few in number; 33 species were weed seeds from fields, presumably brought into the settlement together with the rice harvest, and served as important evidence of rice cultivation at that time.

Other fruits such as kiwis, persimmons, and southern dates found at the Tianluoshan Site were gained from mountains farther away. The distance from the Tianluoshan Site to the southern foot of the Cinan Hills was more than 10 kilometers, but some of the gathering activities would require traveling 20–25 kilometers to the southern ridges, which was likely to take one to two days on foot.

The location of other Hemudu culture sites shared similar characteristics with the Tianluoshan Site. The ancients took into account the biological diversity and the maximization of resources within the area of activity, i.e., a 3–4-hour walking distance to access a variety of resources from different waters, shrub forests, and mountains.

After the locating of the village came the preparation of building materials like timbers and reeds. The cutting and transporting of timbers was the most arduous work. Hundreds of cubic meters of timber was needed for the construction of a stilt long house, and tree felling alone involved a considerable amount of work. The tools for cutting were heavy stone axes, trapezoidal or rectangular in shape, sharpened from the thickest part on both sides, often with sharp asymmetrical edges and chipping marks still visible on the tools. The ax handle was made from a forked branch or horn, with the slender end used as a hand grip. The right half of the lower end of the fork was cut off, and the left half was shaped into a tenon-like binding surface, which could be fitted against the flat upper side of the ax and then tied with a rope or rattan. This method of attachment made it handy for an oblique swing of the tool and increased its effectiveness in tree cutting. The angled chopping marks left by these tools can still be seen on many excavated wooden parts now. The tree felling method was similar to that of a modern man using an iron ax. The stone ax chopped along a circle on the tree truck, first an oblique strike, then a horizontal strike. The repetition of the combination of the two strikes would chop away the wood along the circle piece by piece and form a circular groove in the tree trunk, and a final push or pull would bring the tree down. Archeologists conducted tests with stone axes, in which it took nearly 20 minutes to cut down a tree over 10 centimeters thick. The branches and tops of the felled trees were cut down to reduce the weight as much as possible, and then the logs were transported to the village on the shoulders, pulled back with ropes, or floated there along the streams.

Next, in the village, the people had to work the logs into timber piles, posts, beams, and boards, which required logs to be segmented according to the size of different parts first. The method was roughly the same as tree cutting. The log would be laid flat so that the stone ax could cut a groove along a line and then break the log along it. To process the round cross-section into a square cross-section, stone adzes were also necessary in addition to stone axes. The stone adze was slightly smaller and flatter, with a sharp edge on one side. Its shape was a trapezoid or a long stripe. The handle of the adze was also made of wood or horn, similar in shape to the stone ax handle, but different in the junction with the stone part, in a way that made the tool suitable for shaving and digging. Experts believe that the concave marks on the wood components were caused by the stone adze. Another difficulty arose when large logs had to be cut longitudinally into smaller timbers or plates. According to the traces left on the woodwork and the tools unearthed, stone wedges might have been used, which were similar in shape to stone axes but heavier and with symmetrical edges on both sides. The wedges were used to split the timber in the same way as modern stone wedges are used to split stone plates. At first, wedges were driven into the logs at regular intervals along the longitudinal wood fiber. Each wedge in the log would create a crack. The cracks then joined together to form a through-slit along the grain of the tree. Then the process was repeated on the opposite side of the log. Finally, the wedges were pounded deeper and deeper until the log was completely split. This primitive process to split timber was still used in remote areas such as Tibet and Gansu in modern times, in the absence of saws.

After the logs were cut into timbers and plates, the mortises and tenons had to be made. Stone axes were used to shape tenons, and stone chisels, bone chisels, and horn chisels were used to dig mortises. The finely crafted stone chisels were long, heavy, and single-bladed, with a slightly curved back, but there were also double-bladed chisels. Bone (horn) chisels were made of animal ulna, limb bones, or antlers. Most of the excavated bone (horn) chisels retained the original shape of the bone, with the upper end slightly smoothed and the lower end ground into a sharp double-sided blade. The tops of the chisels were often marked by the pounding of wooden sticks and mallets (槌). But when the wood was not very hard or was newly cut, bone (horn) chisels were sharp enough to dig holes without pounding on the top.

The invention and application of the mortise and tenon joints (榫头), dovetail joints, and rabbet joints in architecture was an outstanding contribution of the Hemudu people, a miracle in the history of Chinese timber architecture, and has had a profound impact on classical Chinese architecture. Apart from timber piles, long round logs, and planks, many wood components with grooves and forked tops were excavated from the Hemudu Site, indicating that many complex junctions were still tied together with ropes. But hundreds of wood components with vertically intersecting mortises and tenons were also unearthed at the Hemudu Site. The types of mortise and tenon include beam tenons, column foot tenons, dovetail tenons, double tenons, blade tenons, and double-fork tenons. Two of these tenons had a 4 : 1 length-to-width ratio, which is a scientific construction structure, later known as the "empirical cross-section". Another tenon had a small circular hole of 3 centimeters in diameter cut in the middle for the insertion of a pin (销钉), called a dowel hole, and its purpose was to prevent the tenon from falling out when the components were stretched. This detail of the tenon proved the maturity of wood construction techniques and the perfection of construction joints to connect beams and columns at the time.

Then how did mortises and tenons work with each other? At the Hemudu Site, mortises were always found on thick columns. Two types of joints were common. For one of them, the beams or timbers were joined horizontally with the help of a middle column. For example, on a thick column with 2 tenons at the same height yet opposite to each other, a rectangular mortise, 9 centimeters long and 7 centimeters wide, was cut at the place 20 centimeters below each tenon, pierced through from both sides, into which the tenons of beams or tie beams could be inserted. This column was later called the "middle column". For another, two wood components were joined with mortise and tenon joints into a right angle, which was seen on a corner column, where the two mortises were cut at right angles to each other at the same height for the tenons of two horizontal beams to be inserted in. In addition, on a square timber, mortises of the same size were cut at equal intervals for the insertion of balusters.

From the descriptions above, several features of the carpentry techniques can be summed up. First, most of the Hemudu mortises and tenons intersected vertically, and the ancient technique of tying was still used at some complex joints. This is evidenced by the grooves for tying on many of the excavated wood components. Second, different technical treatments were devised for components subjected to different forces. Therefore, the forms of mortise and tenon joints were all compliant with the forces they had to bear, and were basically the same as those seen in later wood construction, in spite of their rough appearance due to the rudimentary tools. Third, the use of pins and the invention of the rabbet joint indicated that the Hemudu people had already been remarkably skilled in wood construction.

As the old saying goes, "During human beings' early days, people in the north were cave dwellers and people in the south were nest dwellers." It is a brief summary of the distinctive ancient residential architectural forms of the north and the south. In the chapter "Five Bookworms" of the book *Han Feizi*[①] (《韩非子·五蠹》), it is said that a sage made nest houses on woods to help people avoid the hazards of the beasts, snakes, and worms, and that people were so pleased that they made him king, and called him Youchao (有巢，Nest-Owner). It is beyond our concern whether the account of Youchao as the inventor of the "nest house" is credible. In Chinese history, people did create dwellings on top of big trees in hot and humid swampy areas,

---

① Han Fei or Han Feizi (about 280 BC–233 BC) was an outstanding thinker of the Legalist School (法家) during the Warring States Period, whose works contributed a lot to Emperor Qin Shihuang's rule over China.

which looked like nests from a long distance away. With the development of society, people living in trees gradually moved to the ground. But it was not desirable to build houses directly on wet ground. So, the stilt house emerged. The remains of long houses found in the Hemudu culture indicated Chinese ancestors' admirable house-building techniques about 7,000 years ago.

The architectural remains showed that the foundations of the Hemudu stilt houses consisted of four rows of piles roughly parallel to each other. Three of the rows were set at an interval of 3 meters, and the fourth row was 1.3 meters apart from the third, which was probably for supporting the front porch of the house. So the depth of the house was about 7 meters. The piles, mostly around 0.1 meters in diameter, were driven into the earth at a depth of around 0.5 meters. In each row of piles, several thicker ones were driven 1 meter into the soil at roughly the same intervals. They should be the main load-bearing piles on which the interlocking ground beams were laid. There were two types of joints connecting the piles and the ground beams: for the first type, the thicker piles with forked tops were driven into the earth, and the beams were placed directly on the fork and then tied with ropes; for the second, the advanced technique of mortise and tenon was used to join them, usually with rectangular or concave mortises cut into the upper tip of the thicker piles to fit the tenons of the beams. The floor was then laid on top of the beams. Thus, the base of the elevated dwelling space was formed. Given the height of the residual piles and the thickness of the cultural deposits, the height of the base was approximately 1 meter. The roof truss was then constructed on top. The archeological excavations showed that the roof truss components include columns, beams, tie beams, and purlins. On some wood components, tenons were found at the two ends of the columns and beams, sometimes with dowel holes, meanwhile penetrated mortises in the "middle columns" and orthogonal mortises in the "corner columns" were also discovered. It seemed that mortise and tenon technique was widely used in the roof truss, which was presumed to have been built with several sets of four columns on the elevated base in accordance with the depth. The taller central column was about 3 meters high, the front and rear columns about 2.6 meters high, and the outer column even shorter. Beams were laid on top of the columns. These formed the simplest set of a timber frame, and several such sets constituted a long house. Between two parallel sets, the columns were linked by tie beams, and purlins were placed on the beams and the middle column. The purlins themselves also served to link the frames with mortise and tenon joints. After the construction of the roof truss, the rafters were laid, and the roof was then covered with reed matting and thatch. The space formed by two sets of timber frames is known architecturally as a "room". It is impossible to see with certainty how many "rooms" the Hemudu house typically consisted of. However, the length of the longest row of piles was more than 23 meters, and if the width of each house was 3 meters, the house might have been made up of at least 7–8 rooms, and was undoubtedly a "long house".

The Hemudu stilt houses, built with organic materials like bamboo and wood, was subject to decay. So what the living space and the roof truss above the piles looked like is not known yet. Fortunately, in 2003, a piece of pottery carved with a design of a stilt house excavated at the Xiantanmiao Site (仙坛庙遗址) in Haiyan County provided us with an image of the building. The house design was carved in the center on the inside of the pottery lid. The lower part of the design consisted of six short vertical lines surmounted by a long horizontal line, indicating that each platform was supported by a group of six piles. The upper part of the design had a rather steeply sloping roof, adapted to the local rainy climate. The two slopes were kept in place with a mass of crossed sticks. There were short, thin lines on either side of the roof surface near the ridge, indicating that the roof was paved with thatched hay or straw. The remains of a roof model from the late Liangzhu culture were found at the Bianjiashan Site (卞家山遗址) in Yuhang District, Hangzhou City. The roof plane was rectangular, with steep slopes on four sides and an air window on the upper part of each slope. The surface of the roof was covered with a kind of sloping thin line, a vivid image of the long, thin plant leaves and stems for roof paving. From the above evidence, archeologists inferred the features of the stilt architecture of the Hemudu culture were roughly the same.

The architectural decoration was the final stage in house construction for the Hemudu ancients. The term "decoration" reminds people of the carved beams and painted columns in the Forbidden City in Beijing. In fact, decoration had already sprouted in the Hemudu residential buildings. According to the materials excavated, there were two types of decoration: ornaments on pottery and carvings on wood components. For example, on the front of a pottery block was carved a five-leaved plant in a flowerpot. Another pottery piece was modeled into a small beast with its head turned back. Judging from the size and form of these pottery pieces, archeologists guess that they might have been fitted in some important parts of the building. As for examples of carvings on wood components, on a wooden board with small tenons at both ends, two symmetrical double circles were carved, and on both sides of the circles were carved designs of vertical and diagonal lines. On another board with a flat tenon at each end, an elephant motif was carved. On a third wood component, a large animal was carved, and unfortunately, it was difficult to identify with the head mutilated. These boards, usually tenoned at one or both ends, had probably been inserted into prominent parts of the building.

The primitive village of the Hemudu culture generally consisted of a number of stilt long houses, wooden walls built around the village, and sometimes surrounding rivers outside the walls. The walls consisted of two to three rows of closely arranged piles driven into the earth, some surrounded by rivers, forming the outer defense of the village to protect the safety of the people and livestock. For easy access, wood or bamboo doors were embedded in the walls. Wooden bridges were built over the river outside the village. The roadbeds were reinforced with piles, some with reed mats or reed stalks inserted between the piles, and then paved with pellets of red burned clay, small branches, and pottery fragments.

The Hemudu culture lasted for nearly 1,700 years. During this period, the house-building techniques underwent great changes. In the early phase, stilt houses were built on a one-meter-high elevated base resting on rows of piles driven into the earth. A three-step ladder made of a log was used for the entrance into the house, its lower end was inserted into the ground to prevent movement when people went up or down the ladder, and its side view resembled that of a jag-saw. In the middle phase, the piles for the stilt houses were handled in different ways, either by digging a hole, burying the pile directly into it, and filling the hole with soil, or by digging a hole and placing a wooden board at the bottom and erecting the timber pile on the board. This board was one of the first forms of the column base. In the later phase, the building evolved into a ground house, where the holes were hollowed and then filled with layers of sand, gravel, pottery fragments and red burned clay for reinforcement, forming inverted helmet-like bases. On these bases, wooden columns were erected. There were also cases where the foundation trench for the wall was dug and filled with stones and earth, with the wall built on top. The house began to be divided into different functional areas by earthen walls. At this time the houses were generally built on dry slopes. The walls were reinforced with bamboos and reeds plastered on both inside and outside. The floors were moisture-proof, and in some cases, pits for cooking stoves were dug into the floors. The building techniques of the Hemudu ancients did change a lot during the nearly 1,700 years.

III. A Milestone in Rice Farming

Rice was one of the first food crops to be cultivated and domesticated by man, and it is also the world's most important food crop. Today, more than one-third of the world's population rely on rice as the staple food. There are two species of cultivated rice in the world, namely Asian rice (*Oryza sativa*) and African rice (非洲稻 , *Oryza glaberrima*). Asian cultivated rice originated in the tropical and subtropical regions of Asia, and was cultivated and domesticated from a perennial Asian wild rice. The majority of rice around the world belongs to the Asian cultivated rice, while African cultivated rice is only found in parts of West Africa and some areas of Central and South America. For this reason, the origin of cultivated rice in Asia has naturally become a focus of interest for agronomists all over the world.

The origin of cultivated rice in Asia is widely debated, focusing on the place of origin, the time of origin, and the rice species. Some believe that India was the place of origin while China and the rest of Asia functioned only as a "secondary center". They mainly draw on evidence that India has many variants of wild rice. Chinese agronomists believe that cultivated rice in China originated locally, but opinions differ as to where it originated. After the discovery of a large number of rice remains from the Hemudu culture, Chinese experts began to speculate on the origin of cultivated rice based on the archeological findings. Various hypotheses have been put forward, including the South China Theory, the Lower Yangtze River Region Theory, the Middle Yangtze River Region Theory, and the Middle and Lower Yangtze River Region Theory.

As to when rice cultivation began, opinions are also divided. Some believe that it started in the legendary "Shennong[1] Era". Some scholars believe that it can be traced back to about 10,000 years ago, the early Neolithic Period.

On the issue of rice species, the debate is still heated. Some scholars have concluded that wild indica in South China was the ancestor of the cultivated rice, and that in the process of northward spreading, japonica split from the earliest cultivated species–indica. It has also been suggested that japonica originated in the Yangtze River Region, while indica may have originated in South Asia, such as India, based on the observation and analysis of wild rice in Chaohu County, Anhui Province. Although the origin of cultivated rice has been explored for nearly a hundred years, the debate continues. The discovery of cultivated rice at the Hemudu Site in 1973 has lent a new dimension to the debate and has led the issue to a more in-depth discussion.

By the Late Paleolithic Period, primitive people had gradually mastered the growth rules of some plants during their gathering and hunting activities, and discovered that the seeds or tuberous roots of some plants could germinate, grow, and bear fruit in the right climate, moisture, and soil. Inspired by this, they gradually began to experiment with artificial care and cultivation of plants in suitable places near their dwellings on purpose. Thus, the first agriculture emerged, and society entered the Neolithic Age, a new era where food was mainly gained from what people grew. The origins of primitive agriculture (原始农业) in China can be traced back at least to 10,000 years ago, and it developed from the primitive stage of slash-and-burn (刀耕火种) cultivation to the more advanced stage of "hoe-tillage" (锄耕) or "*si*-tillage" (耜耕) about 7,000 years ago. Consequently, human settlement became more stable.

Remains of rice cultivation were found in many sites of the Hemudu

---

[1]   *Shennong* (神农) was a legendary figure, a holy forefather of the Chinese, who was believed to have lived about 6,000 years ago and have invented agriculture and discovered the curative virtues of plants. The Chinese character *shen* (神) means a god, and the Chinese character *nong* (农) means agriculture.

culture, indicating that rice was already a staple food for the people. The Hemudu Site was definitely the site with the richest rice remains, followed by the Tianluoshan Site. Dark brown organic deposits were found in the two excavations of the Hemudu Site. Superimposition of them with layers of green, yellow, white, and greenish-grey fine sand resulted in more than 10 layers, which were vividly called the sandwiched layers. The thickness of these layers varied from 10 to 60 centimeters, with an average of 40–50 centimeters. They consisted mainly of reed stems and leaves, rice stems and leaves, husks, and wood chips. In some places, there were superimposed layers of husks. The color of stalks, leaves, and husks was bright yellow when they were unearthed. The husks maintained a good shape, with clearly discernible veins and glume hairs. And some rice ears were still attached to the stalks. But the remains turned black in a flash after being unearthed. At the same time, charred rice grains could be seen in some of the ashes and burned wood residues. Inside many pottery *fu*, there were often burned rice grains or rice crusts on the bottom. On the inner wall of the greenware of charcoal-tempered pottery, the shape of rice husks was also discernible. On the belly of a pottery basin was carved the rice pattern, with rice ears standing upright in the middle and heavy grains dropping down to the sides, next to which was a carved pig image (most of it was missing), a true depiction of the more developed rice farming and livestock breeding of the time. Such sandwiched layers were also excavated in the Tianluoshan Site. Interestingly, several piles of empty husks were found at the site, mostly less than 1 square meter in area and 2–10 centimeters in depth, possibly the waste from grain hulling. Fewer whole grains were excavated in the Tianluoshan Site than in the Hemudu Site. But large quantities of hulled grains were unearthed there. Similarly, the majority of rice remains at the sites of Zishan, Tongjia'ao, and Fujiashan were also hulled grains, while few rice grains with hulls were found.

The substantial amount and the good preservation of rice found in the Hemudu culture were unprecedented in previous Neolithic sites and aroused great interest among archeologists and agronomists. But the essential question that agronomists wanted to explore was whether the rice was cultivated or wild.

Though evolved from wild rice, the cultivated rice differs from the wild species in many aspects. First, the grains of ordinary wild rice are smaller and slender, while grains of cultivated rice are longer and larger and weigh more. Second, only some immature and blighted grains of wild rice will still be attached to the stalk, while the ripened grains will fall off by themselves. In contrast, grains on a cultivated rice ear tend to ripen at about the same time and are collected before they fall by themselves. Third, the pollen of cultivated rice is generally larger than that of wild rice, though there is no strict distinction between these two. Fourth, the plants of cultivated rice are larger than the wild ones. The variation in the traits of cultivated rice has been the result of long-term artificial selection and breeding. According to these distinctions, the rice unearthed in the Hemudu culture was identified as cultivated rice for the following reasons. For one thing, the pollen grains discovered at Hemudu were generally around 30 micrometers in diameter, with the largest reaching 49.48 micrometers, much larger than the wild pollen. For another, the rice grains found in the Hemudu culture were longer and larger, and weighed far more than the wild rice grains. Apart from the morphological differences, the rice found in the layers of the Hemudu culture was often piled up with stalks and leaves. This was a piece of further evidence, for if the rice had been collected from the wild, only the ears would have been harvested, not the roots, stems, or leaves.

Was the Hemudu rice indica or japonica? A number of morphological and physiological factors can distinguish indica rice from japonica rice, such as the grain shape, glume hairs, grain color, leaf shape, and tiller capacity. Due to the age of the grains from the Hemudu culture, many tests were no longer applicable, and the only way to identify them was to examine their shape (through measuring the grain length and width and the calculation of the aspect ratio) and the distribution of glume hairs, a highly reliable method advocated by agronomists. In this way, two types of rice from the Hemudu culture were identified, one with smaller grains and the other with larger grains. The smaller grains had an aspect ratio of 2.71, while the larger grains had an aspect ratio of 2.53, with an average of 2.62. Both were consistent with the aspect ratio of indica rice, ranging from 2 to 3, generally above 2. In contrast, the aspect ratio of japonica rice ranges from 1.6 to 2.3, generally below 2. In terms of glume hairs, the glume hairs of the Hemudu rice, which were of the same length, evenly distributed, and neatly arranged, was more in line with the characteristics of indica rice. The glume hairs of japonica rice are of different lengths and unevenly distributed, to be specific, concentrated in the upper part of the glumes but sparsely distributed in the lower part. Further measurements of the whole grains confirmed that the Hemudu cultivated rice was a mixture of indica rice and japonica rice, with the former accounting for 60.32% and the latter 39.68%. Now came the conclusion that the Hemudu rice was a relatively primitive heterogeneous group of indica rice and japonica rice, for an obvious variation existed in the grain length and width of both, and there were also a small number of intermediate types with some resemblance with both.

Was the Hemudu rice cultivated from wild rice in the lower Yangtze River Region? Was there wild rice in the lower Yangtze River Region? Nowadays, it is difficult to find traces of wild rice due to long-term development in this area, for wild rice, considered a weed, has been constantly removed over the years. But Tang Shengxiang (汤圣祥), Yoichiro Sato (佐藤洋一郎), and Yu Weijie (俞为洁) found four grains of wild rice out of 105 rice grains with the help of electron microscopic scanning. when studying the sub-micro structure (亚微结构) of charred grains of the Hemudu rice. It seemed that the ancients also collected wild rice while cultivating rice. Therefore, it was proved that about 7,000 years ago, wild rice grew in Ningbo. This undoubtedly provided the prerequisites for the domestication of wild rice by the primitive inhabitants of this region. This conclusion was further evidenced by the discovery of rice farming remains from more than 10,000 years ago in Zhejiang Province, such as at the Shangshan Site in Pujiang County and the Xiaohuangshan Site in Shengzhou County, thus pushing the upper limit of rice farming in Zhejiang Province to the Neolithic Period, i.e. more than 10,000 years ago, and also proving the lower reaches of the Yangtze River as one of the origins of rice cultivation in China. Meanwhile, Japanese agricultural scientists studied the distribution and evolution of rice varieties across Asia using phenolase isozyme electrophoresis (酚酶同功 酶电泳法), and their findings proved that the southwestern and southern regions of China were centers of rice mutation. This is another evidence from modern science that the lower Yangtze River Region, including Ningbo, was one of the birthplaces of cultivated rice in China.

The numerous and diverse production tools found in the Hemudu culture can be divided into four types according to their materials: stone tools such as stone axes, stone adzes, stone chisels, stone grinding plates, stone grinding sticks, and stone knives; bone tools such as bone *si*, bone arrowheads, bone whistles, and bone fish darts; pottery tools like pottery spindle whorls, pottery paddles, and pottery mortars (陶臼); and wooden tools like wooden dibbles, wooden *si*, wooden pestles, wood grinding plates, and wood grinding sticks. Among them, the bone *si* (骨耜), the wood *si*, the stone knife and the wood dibble were supposed to specialize in agricultural production then.

The bone *si* was one of the typical objects of the Hemudu culture. More than 200 pieces were found, mostly made from the scapulae of cattle and deer. Their shapes basically retained the natural forms of the scapulae, with only simple processing, like cutting off the protruding part of the scapular spine and smoothing the top of the shoulder socket. The surface was smooth and shiny from long-term use, with numerous friction marks visible to the naked eye near the cutting part. A shallow longitudinal groove was cut in the middle of the bone plate with an oblong hole on each side of the lower part of the groove and a rectangular hole on each side of the upper part of the groove. There were traces of long-term cordage binding around these holes. At the sites of Hemudu and Tianluoshan was found a bone *si* tied to a small section of a wooden handle with multiple loops of rattan, suggesting that they were fitted with vertical wooden handles. Its lower end was cut at an angle to match the shallow groove and tied at the four holes with rattan, with the upper end of the handle carved into a triangle or a T-shape for ease of handling. The restored bone *si* resembled the modern shovels still in use in southern China.

Since its discovery, the use of the bone *si* has attracted much attention from the archeological and agricultural history communities, but opinions are still divided. There are three types of *si* of the Hemudu culture according to the shape of the lower end: bifurcated, beveled-bladed, and flat-edged. Their functions were also different. The bifurcated type, according to foreign ethnographic literature, might have been used to process animal hides and skins. To confirm that, archeologists used modern buffalo scapulae to imitate the bifurcated bone *si* and observed the subtle marks left on it after processing animal hides and plant fibers, and then compared the marks with the traces of use left on the bifurcated bone *si* of the Hemudu culture. Its function as a tool for animal hide and plant fiber processing was confirmed. However, apart from traces of use on the forked part of the unearthed bifurcated *si,* its furcated front was sharpened to a single edge and also showed the same fine friction marks of prolonged use as those on the beveled and flat-edged *si.* So came the next question: was the bifurcated bone *si* also used for farming? The archeologists conducted further experiments with the modern replicas, such as using them to remove reeds and weeds in ponds and marshes, to dig rice paddies, and to dig the topsoil, cultural layers, and greenish-grey silt in the site. The results showed that the buffalo scapula was not as fragile as it was originally thought to be and could well withstand digging strokes. The replicas were more than adequate for removing reeds and weeds or digging up mud, as long as they did not hit something very hard, such as a stone, and were significantly more efficient at digging up the water-soaked rice paddies than at digging up dry soil. When digging harder soil, stepping a foot on the smooth socket of the *si* would significantly increase labor efficiency. And the replica of flat-edged *si,* with a shorter, narrower, and flatter blade, was more handy and effective than the other two in digging up soil. So, the answer to the question is: the different types of the bone *si* were all likely to have been used in agricultural production.

In ancient Chinese documents, there are many records about *lei* (耒, a farming tool for dibbling and digging holes), and *si.* According to these records, both *lei* and *si* were composite agricultural production tools (复合型农业生产工具) made of wood. Unearthed at both the Tianluoshan Site and the Cihu Site, some 60–80 centimeters long single pointed wooden sticks fit for hand grip, which archeologists referred to as dibbles, were possibly the ancient "*lei*". Along with these findings and the excavation of the Hemudu bone *si,* a fact was further proved: the agricultural stage when *lei* and *si* made of not only wood but also animal bones were used for farming did exist in ancient China.

Then how did the Hemudu people cultivate rice about 7,000 years ago? The survey and drilling showed that paddies were located close to the primitive villages, on the edge of low-lying lakes and swamps, with around 100 acres for each village. At that time, people did not have the same field plots and supporting irrigation facilities (配套水利灌溉设施) for rice cultivation as today. So they used the mudflats of the lakes and swamps to grow rice. Before planting, the Hemudu people used the bone *si* to remove reeds and weeds from the fields, level the land, turn over the soil, make ditches, and dig pits. In the late phase of the Hemudu culture, the wooden *si,* which had the same shape and function as the bone *si,* replaced the bone *si* as the main farming tool.

Paddy management is much more complex than dry-land farming in the north. For one thing, rice is a water-loving crop that requires timely irrigation and draining. For another, the fields have to be plowed and weeded timely.

How did they harvest rice then? When the season came, the Hemudu ancients would probably hold some religious rituals to pray for a good harvest, as they did not yet understand various natural phenomena and hoped to dominate nature through supernatural power. Then rice ears were cut off near the root with tools like knives or sickles, which could be evidenced by the piles of rice, husks, stalks, and leaves excavated at the sites of the Hemudu culture. Then what were the tools like? Bone tools with serrated edge were excavated and named after their shapes, such as serrated tools, saw-shaped tools, and sickle-shaped tools. The tools were slightly curved, with the front either pointed or rounded and the rear much mutilated in many cases, and the lower side processed into serrations at approximately equal intervals slightly slanted towards the rear. Because of the resemblance in shape between them and the later scythes, they are assumed to be tools for rice harvesting. But this is only a guess of the past based on the standards and conditions of today, for in some areas populated by national minorities, the "bone scythe" was used as a primitive tool for kneading leather. Thus, experts were not sure of the use of the "bone scythes" excavated in Hemudu culture. So, what tools did they use for rice harvesting? Another type of tools was found in the Hemudu culture — a number of finely ground rectangular stone knives, with rounded corners, two pierced round holes, and flat blades on both sides, but unfortunately parts of the implement were missing. A cord was likely to have been threaded through the holes to attach the stone knives to the fingers, and thus it could be used to cut the rice ears. Their blades were blunted after being used for a long period. As a result, sometimes the stalks were inevitably taken together with the ears. That is why the rice stalks and leaves were interspersed in the piles of rice. These stone knives were the precursors to the ancient sickles. In the chapter "Guangwu" (广物) of the ancient dictionary *Xiao'erya* — (《 小尔雅 》, *The Dictionary of Names of Things*), it is said, "The ears of the grain are called *ying* (颖), and the tool for cutting *ying* is called *zhi* (铚，sickle)." In addition, in the Hemudu culture there were also knife-shaped tools made from split pig tusks, short and tied to a small wooden handle, with a single blade on the outer arc of the tusk, presumably also capable of harvesting rice.

From the above-mentioned remains of rice and rice cultivation, it can be judged that the farming techniques (耕作技术) were relatively advanced and the yield was considerable, far more than that in the primary agricultural stage. Accordingly, we believe that, on the basis of their long experience in rice cultivation, the Hemudu ancients must have mastered preliminary knowledge of the farming seasons and even some astronomical knowledge, which contributed to the development of primitive agriculture. The development of production tools is an objective measure of the development of social productivity. The bone and wooden *si* to cultivate the land and the tools made of bones, stones, and mussel shells for rice harvesting marked a relatively advanced stage in the development of Hemudu agriculture.

IV. Domestication of Dogs and Pigs

Domestic animals were tamed from their wild ancestors. However, this process was not accomplished in one stroke. The first thing was to tame wild animals, to transform them into controllable and submissive ones. After that, there was a lengthy process of domestication to adapt them to domestic conditions, during which these animals would be constantly selected and bred. In the long process of domestication, humans found that not all tamed animals were suitable for domestic use, and that only a few species could serve as livestock in the long run, for some of them would lose the ability to reproduce once kept in captivity. Animal breeding, as well as grain cultivation, is often regarded as a great breakthrough of epoch-making significance in the history of mankind.

Then how did domestication begin? When human society was first shaped, the ancients lived an extremely hard nomadic life. Hunting, fishing, and gathering (for example, picking fruits, digging up tuberous roots, and grabbing eggs from the nests) were their means of life. With their accumulated experience in hunting, the number of prey grew constantly over time. Sometimes, they captured so many beasts that they could not consume them all at once. To deal with this, they came up with a new idea — to keep and feed the slightly injured, the uninjured, or the cubs. During this process, they gradually discovered that some animals were close to humans and could be tamed and bred. Thus, they started selecting and mating these animals on purpose. Generation after generation, domestic animals finally came into being.

The numbers and species of animal remains discovered at the Hemudu Site are striking. Preliminary data suggest that there were 61 species in total, including primates, artiodactyls, proboscideans, carnivorans, rodents, pangolins, birds, reptiles and fishes. Most of them were common mammals such as dogs, pigs, cattle, deer, and monkeys. But rare animals like rhinoceros and elephants were also found. Only dogs and pigs were domestic.

It is generally believed that the dog was one of the species first domesticated, whose domestication can date back to the Paleolithic Period. Wolves, the ancestors of dogs, wandered over the places now named Asia, Africa, Europe, and America. Hunters would often steal the cubs while adult wolves were absent from the dens and then breed them in their own settlements. However, the domestication could not be completed in a short time. The first step was to tame the wolves, substituting docility for their ferocity while keeping their inherent alertness, agility, keenness, and agility in pursuing prey. To achieve this, our ancestors selected some tamed ones, bred them, and trained them consistently. Despite the fact that dogs descended from wolves, the differences in their bulk, skeleton, and habits become distinct with the passage of time. The wolf has bigger muscles, stronger bones, a longer skull, and sharper teeth, especially the canine teeth on their upper gums. However, the dog, whose territory is constricted due to artificial rearing, has vestigial muscles and bones, a shorter skull, and a broader snout. Its teeth have also degenerated. The canine teeth and the carnassial teeth are not as robust and sharp as those of the wolf's, as a result of its evolution from a carnivorous animal into an omnivorous one.

More than 10 intact dog skulls were found at the Hemudu Site, which were small in size and featured a sunken tip of the nasal bone, small and flat otocysts, smooth posterior margin of the back nasal crest, reduced sagittal crests, irretroflex cristas, slightly arched bottoms of lower jaws, weak carnassial teeth and canine teeth. These characteristics were obviously different from those of the wolves and closer to those of modern domestic dogs, indicating that the Hemudu people had already domesticated dogs. More convincingly, a large amount of dog feces was found in the residential area, containing a large number of recognizable bone fragments of animals, mainly fish, further proving their domestication of dogs.

Dogs were raised for many purposes. Firstly, dogs could function as a "food reserve" (储备粮) to pull through poor harvests and temporary shortages. Secondly, dogs were their "followers" and "assistants" in hunting, for at that time, there were numerous wild animals to be hunted in dense forests, lakes, and swamps around the village. Moreover, as large rice paddies were close to lakes or swamps, dogs became the guards on crops from the devastating damage caused by birds and wild animals living there, especially when the harvest season came. Finally, dogs became their loyal guards against the sudden attacks of predators. Though the villagers used wood piles to form a wall around the village and lived in the stilt houses to stay away from the harm of snakes and insects, large predators were still a threat. But dogs could fend off their attacks.

What was domesticated next to the dog was the pig. According to research, pigs in many places have been domesticated from local wild boars. For example, the European pig and the Asian pig were domesticated from the local wild boar respectively. Now, pigs in North China are similar to wild boars in north China, and pigs in South China are similar to those in South China.

At the Hemudu Site, many skeletons of both pigs and wild boars have been unearthed. Now, we have learned the difference between these two species. Wild boars, which usually live in the mountains, grasslands, and swamps, have a slimmer body and thin limbs allowing them to move swiftly. Their snout is long and powerful, suitable for digging soil either for food or nests in the ground. They have powerful canine teeth, a straight head position, and well-developed forequarters. The ratio of forequarters to hindquarters is about 7 : 3. However, after long-term artificial feeding, the head of modern pigs has degenerated, the snout shorter, the hindquarters more developed, and the waist and back broader. The ratio of forequarters to hind quarters is about 3 : 7. The limbs become shorter and thinner. Their movement is not swift, and their canine teeth have degenerated. As for the

many boar bones unearthed at the Hemudu Site, the skull was complete
and characterized by a long snout, a low and flat forehead, complex molar
teeth, and strong canine teeth. Most of the bones of pigs were broken and
incomplete; the skull was characterized by a short snout, a wide forehead,
slightly outward sloping cheekbones, deep sunken cheeks, and triangular
lacrimal bones. The pig and the boar were distinctly different in the structure
of bones. According to the abrasion of teeth, the number of adult pigs was
predominant, followed by that of cubs, while the number of old ones was
the least. This can be justified by the fact that animals usually reach a stable
maximum weight near maturity, when slaughtering them can maximize the
gain of meat. So most domesticated animals die at a predominantly young
age. The majority of the remains of pigs found at the Hemudu Site belonged
to young and adult ones, indicating that these pigs were probably artificially
fattened and slaughtered for food.

A very cute pottery pig with a short snout, a fat belly, and short thick
limbs was unearthed at the Hemudu Site. The ratio of its forequarters to the
hindquarters is about 1 : 1. This is undoubtedly an important evidence that
the Hemudu pig raised by the villagers was still in transition from the wild
boar to the modern pig. In addition, there is a rectangular *bo* with rounded
corners. On each of its long sides, a pig was carved respectively, with a
long snout, erect ears, long legs, a short tail, a coarse mane, and a slightly
drooping belly. The image is really vivid. Another turtle-shaped pottery
utensil named *he* was carved with 6 animal images, 5 of which are pigs, all
with a long snout, upright ears, slim legs, a long tail, a coarse mane, a thin
and long waist, resembling the figure of wild boars.

In addition to dogs and pigs, were the ancients of Hemudu domesticating
or raising other animals? Judging from the shapes of the unearthed bones,
it is difficult to draw a conclusion. However, it is worth noting that deer
skeletons were unearthed in considerable numbers. More than 500 pieces of
Père David's elk horns were unearthed at the Hemudu Site, but only one was
intact. Most belonged to young elk and were ripped off instead of falling off

by themselves as the result of their growth. Therefore, it might be assumed that the Hemudu people domesticated them. Other facts may also support this assumption. For one thing, elks were found in large numbers at many other sites of that time; for another, their domestication did occur in history later. Moreover, a number of bone whistles were found, some of which can still make sound. Archeologists and artists believe that bone whistles might have been used to hunt or domesticate animals, elks for instance. But the conclusion has not been made yet, as the evidence from the unearthed bones is insufficient.

Some buffalo bones were unearthed at the Hemudu Site, among which 16 pieces of relatively complete skull were identified as those of short-horned water buffaloes (*Bubalus mephistopheles*) by paleozoologists, according to the shapes of horns and the skull. These short-horned water buffaloes were previously thought to be the world's first domesticated buffaloes. However, the research shows that the short-horned water buffaloes unearthed at sites such as Kuahuqiao, Hemudu and Luojiajiao in Zhejiang Province were all wild and were gained from hunting by ancient people. The modern domestic buffalo was domesticated from the wild swamp buffalo in South Asia (南亚野生沼泽水牛), which is quite different from the short-horned water buffalo in shape. The age of death among the short-horned water buffalo at the Hemudu Site was different from that among the domesticated breeds, and this state remained throughout the Neolithic Age, which suggests no evidence of domestication. Although not domesticated, the short-horned water buffaloes of Hemudu were large in shape and gentle in temperament. It was very likely that the ancients drove them into the farmland after a little domestication and let them trample the land to achieve the effect of weeding and soil turning.

Moreover, a pottery sheep was unearthed at the Hemudu Site. Its head is small, the neck thick and short, the limbs short, and the body fat, wide and slightly long. Although small, the pottery sheep has a realistic image and is very attractive. These characteristics naturally make people associate it with home sheep and take it as evidence that the Hemudu ancients raised sheep. But sheep bones were found in small numbers and incomplete, making it difficult to tell if they were domesticated.

V. Gathering, Fishing and Hunting

About 7,000 years ago, the Hemudu people already stopped the barbaric life of eating raw food and started a relatively stable life in settlements, with their rice farming developed to the *si*-tillage stage (耙耕农业阶段). However, due to limited productivity, people were unable to resist natural disasters, and the yield of rice farming was very low—even lower in the face of various natural disasters. So there must have been other economic activities to supplement agricultural harvests, namely gathering, fishing and hunting.

Gathering was still one of the most important sources of food for the Hemudu ancients. Archeological excavations often reveal many fruits, kernels, seeds, mushrooms, and mollusk shells. These diverse remains were found in great numbers, some in piles and pits, with the largest piles reaching hundreds of pounds. They were also very well preserved. Many acorns were still attached to their pedicels. Even mushrooms, which were hard to preserve when they were fresh, still retained their original appearance.

Many edible plants were found in the Hemudu culture. The main species include acorns, water chestnuts, Gorgon fruit, jujubes, acacia seeds, and grains of Job's tears. Starch-rich fruit, namely the first three of the above, was the majority. Often piles of acorns and water chestnuts were excavated, some intact, some in broken shells, which might have been stored after collection or discarded after consumption. The bottle gourds were bright yellow when they were found, and it is assumed that some were collected in the wild and some were cultivated. The ripe bottle gourds, with thick skins, could be dried to make ladles. There were also a lot of camphor leaves, which filled one pottery jar in one case. But there was very little camphor pollen on the site, suggesting that camphors were collected from afar and brought back by people. But it is worth exploring whether the inhabitants already knew how to use them to guard against insects and disease. The late Harvard University professor Kwang-chih Chang (张光直) once said the people at the Hemudu Site were "affluent foragers"[1]. Food gathering prepared the preconditions for the starting and development of agriculture. The American scholar Mr. Sauer suggested, "Agriculture did not originate from a long-term lack of food. People lived in famine did not have the means or the time to engage in the leisurely and time-consuming experiments to develop a better and different kind of food only in the distant future, or select plants to make them more useful to mankind. Only people who led a life considerably different from famine were able to farm."[2] It was during their long-term gathering activities that the Hemudu ancients became familiar with the growth patterns of some plants and tried to cultivate them. And it was in this context that rice farming emerged.

Generally, women and children were the ones to dig up wild vegetables and underground tuberous roots (stems), or pick mushrooms, given the small sphere of the gathering activities and the low physical effort involved. However, when we studied the plants, it turned out that the collection time for most fruits and seeds, such as the acorns, jujubes, and water chestnuts, concentrated from August to October, coinciding with the rice harvest season. And some had a very short collection time; for example, ripe water chestnuts floated in water only for less than ten days before sinking to the bottom, and ripe acorns stayed on trees for only about one to three weeks before falling. In such a case, it was not enough to rely only on women and children. Often the whole village — men, women and children — all had to work. The people, carrying reed baskets or corded pottery pots, were divided into several groups, some going up the mountain and others to the rice paddies. Fruits

---

① 张光直. 中国东南海岸的 "富裕的食物采集文化" [J]. 上海博物馆集刊，1987 (0)：143-149.

② Sauer, C O. *Agricultural Origins and Dispersals* [M]. New York: American Geographical Society, 1952.

and seeds were brought back to the settlements in a steady stream. In order to preserve them for a longer time, on sunny days, people dried them on reed mats or under the sunny eaves, then stored them in pottery pots and basins, or in pits with reed mats underneath, and then covered them with reed mats. These pits functioned similarly to today's cellars. Their storage capacity was really huge. For example, at the Tianluoshan Site, a third of the acorn storage from one pit alone filled two large buckets brought by the archeologists.

As a natural economy, fishing and hunting was the lifeblood of humankind in the distant Paleolithic Period. By about 7,000 years ago, people had already accumulated rich experience in fishing and hunting, still a necessary supplement to the agricultural economy. In the early layer of the Hemudu culture, so many broken pieces of various animal remains were scattered around the settlement that they had to be counted in tons. The bones were discarded by the ancients after they had sucked out the marrow. And some were scrap pieces from tool making. By incomplete statistics, the animal remains unearthed at the Hemudu Site belonged to 61 species and genera, 58 vertebrate species, including birds, reptiles, fish, and mammals, and only 3 invertebrate species. Mammals accounted for the most, 34 species to be exact. Of course, not all of these animals were obtained from fishing and hunting for food, nor did they make up the whole of the edible wild animals. The animal skeletons from the Tianluoshan Site were also relatively well preserved, including wild boars, pigs, short-horned water buffaloes, elks, sambar deer, sika deer, Siberian weasels, water deer, dogs, badgers, masked palm civets, yellow-throated martens otters, monkeys, large and small Indian civets, Asiatic black bears, and leopards, most of which were also seen at the Hemudu Site. According to the number of animal remains, the people's main source of meat was aquatic animals. There were so many remains of fish, turtles, and other aquatic animals unearthed in the archeological excavations that it was impossible to count or distinguish all of them. The discovery of sea creature remains like those of tunas, sharks, whales, and sea turtles further evidenced the development of fishing and the important contribution of fishing to their meat diet. Excavations at the Tianluoshan Site and Zishan Site often revealed layers of fish scales, and fish bones under charcoal chips or in pits of different sizes. From one pit, which is 80 centimeters long, 60 centimeters wide, and 40 centimeters deep, more than 1,500 fish, mainly carp, 35–45 centimeters in length, were identified, according to the examination of the pharyngeal dentary. The second largest group were wild herbivores like the elk and sika deer. In addition, the forest-dwelling animals accounted for but a small proportion of the total. The identification of specimen suggested that given the ancients' limited hunting ability, two methods might have been used to catch animals that were fierce, huge, or good at running: to catch prey from the weaker species instead of the strong, or to choose prey from large resistless herds. In short, fishing was the main source of meat for the Hemudu ancients, followed by hunting in the grasslands, while hunting activities for fierce animals like tigers in the mountains were rare.

What kind of tools did the Hemudu ancients use for fishing and hunting? The tools were diversified, including bone arrowheads, bone whistles, bone fish darts, bows, wooden spears, wooden sticks, etc. Stone balls, pottery pellets and stone pellets could also be used for hunting

Their most common hunting tool was the composite tool of the bow and arrow. The bow was generally made of wood, and the bowstring might have been made from animal sinew or plant rattan. One thumb-thin bow made of hardwood was excavated, slightly bent, already broken in one end, with a roughly square cross-section. On the well-preserved end, there was a groove for tying the bowstring. The invention and use of the bow and arrow had the advantage of a longer range, faster speed, and a higher hit rate compared with other primitive tools. Its invention and use made prey within the range from dozens away to hundreds of meters away within the human reach.

The arrow consisted of an arrowhead and a shaft. Many small round wood sticks found at the Hemudu Site may have been arrow shafts. Most of the arrowheads were made from animal bones, and as easily consumed tools, they were made in particularly large numbers and accounted for the majority of the unearthed relics. For example, at the Hemudu Site, 1,780 pieces of the 6,700 excavated artifacts were bone arrowheads, and at the Tianluosan Site, the number of bone arrowheads accounted for almost more than half of all the excavated artifacts. These bone arrowheads were generally about 10 centimeters long, a few only 5–6 centimeters, while several 15 centimeters or longer. Due to the different materials and uses, they were generally made in three shapes. The first type, shaped like a flat thin willow leaf, was processed by inserting the joint end of the bone arrowhead (hereinafter referred to as "tang") directly into the shaft. Its sharp edge was able to penetrate animal hides and cause remarkable lethality. Because of its simple processing method and tremendous killing power, this type was the most numerous. The second type's tang was shaped into long slanting surfaces, often carved with a shallow groove to combine with the arrow shaft, whose end was cut to a corresponding angle. When the two were well integrated, the low resistance, stable gravity center, and fast speed would make the shot more accurate. The third type had a conical tang. The majority of this type had a sharp arrow front while some a blunt one, which suggests the latter was used only in exceptional circumstances. Then, what were the circumstances? Why were they made blunt? If the purpose of hunting was to get the beautiful feathers of a bird or the fine fur of a small beast, it was necessary to ensure the prey was intact and free from bloodstain when caught. The blunt arrows could cause internal injuries to the prey without damaging its appearance. It is said that nowadays hunters in some parts of South China still use this method for this purpose.

Long and slender wooden spears, made of hardwood, with sharp blades, were found in small numbers. The end of the spear was cut thinner and sometimes carved with grooves to make it easy to bind with a wooden handle. Generally, it was thrown out by hand. But it could also be shot with the help of the bow and arrow. There were also bone spears, apart from wooden ones.

Over 100 bone whistles were unearthed, second in number to bone arrowheads. Take a hollow section of a bird's limb, such as that of a goose or duck, then grind a few small holes with a grindstone, and a bone whistle is finished. Usually, the bone whistle had one hole at each end, but bone whistles with one or three or four holes were also found. Sometimes, hollow wild boar tusks or tusks of smaller animals were used to make bone whistles. In order to make more varied sounds, a particularly clever inventor inserted a bone stick into the cavity of the whistle, which could be pulled rhythmically to make different tunes. Most common bone whistles, though, could also play different tunes by pressing and releasing a finger on the small holes. In the past, the whistle was thought to be a child's toy for fun. Others thought it was a musical instrument (a flute). More recently, it was seen as a tool for separating warp yarns on a primitive weaving machine, based on signs of wear and tear. In our modern experience, the bone whistle is a musical instrument for pure reaction, but it was likely to have played a greater role in hunting activities. During the Hemudu culture, despite the favorable environment and the abundance of natural produce, people were not always favored by nature, and their lives were far from the abundance of food and clothing that we might expect. For most of the time, they had to struggle for survival. So their initial motivation for making each object was to make a living, and the bone whistle was no exception. According to ethnographic sources, all animals have their own "language" and they react differently to various sounds. If a stray animal hears the call of its companions, it will run to join the herd; if a weaker animal hears the call of its natural predator, it will flee; if a fierce animal hears the call of its prey, it will immediately get ready for an attack; and some animals will lure the opposite sex with their calls during the rut. In all these cases, communication is made through sound. The Hemudu people gradually learned the animal "languages" after having dealings with them for a long time. Therefore, they invented a tool — the bone whistle — to imitate the different sounds of birds and animals, so as to trap them. To ensnare animals by sound was often used in primitive societies. The Ewenki people living in the northeast of China used to blow wooden whistles to lure deer out, and then shoot them with guns or arrows when they got closer. Similarly, the bone whistles in the Hemudu culture might have been used to aid hunting.

Stone balls, as large as fists or as small as eggs, were also their hunting tools, but only a small number of them were found. There were several ways to use them. For example, a long rope was attached to the stone ball on one end and to a long wooden pole on the other end. When the pole was thrown, the stone ball leaped out and spun rapidly after hitting the target, and thus the beast's limbs were bound firmly by the rope. In another way, one end of the rope was attached to the stone ball and the other was held in hand. The stone ball was first swung to make it spin and then thrown out to knock down the beast, in the same way the chain ball is thrown in sports nowadays.

Pellets made of pottery and stone were their common hunting tools as well. A slingshot was used to fire a pellet: the user placed the pellet in the band, held the band, pulled the string, and fired the pellet. The Jingpo people in Yunnan used to make slingshots from bamboo slips, and strings from withes, with a net attached for pellet shooting. And the Dai people used similar slingshots.

The bone fish dart was made from the tubular bones of a large or medium-sized animal. It was long and flat, with a sharp edge and barbed sides. Once embedded in the fish, the barbs penetrated deep, making it difficult for the fish to escape. However, only three or four such bone fish darts were found, far from proving them as common fishing tools of the time.

Armed with only primitive hunting tools like bows and arrows, wooden spears, pellets, and bone whistles, the Hemudu ancients could not guarantee a fruitful return every time. With these nonlethal weapons, it was really not easy to catch huge, fierce animals good at running, such as tigers, bears, and rhinoceroses. In such cases where they were unable to win by force, they had to take wisely. The first step was to choose animals that were weak, numerous, and moving in herds. For example, the deer were exactly the choice. About 7,000 years ago, the Yuyao-Cicheng Plain was full of lakes and marshes, an ideal place for deer to play. Moreover, deer could be hunted with bows and arrows, stone balls, wooden spears, sticks, and even with bare hands. Second, they chose to avoid the strong and catch the weak. The old, the weak, the disabled, or the young were their choices when they attacked the fierce animals. Through identification, experts found most of the rhinoceroses excavated were still with milk teeth, indicating that they were cubs, easier to catch than adult rhinoceros; some rhinoceroses, with their teeth indicating serious diseases, might have belonged to the old and the sick. Third, traps were set. The vast expanse of waters surrounding the village, like lakes and swamps, were natural traps. A group of people would take advantage of the terrain and work together to drive the animals into the lakes and swamps before catching them. Finally, they made use of winter as a good hunting opportunity. Some animals slowed down and some others started hibernation in winter, making them vulnerable to attack. (Today, when wild boars, pheasants, and muntjacs go out for food in the snow, they often enter farmhouses by mistake and are caught by villagers.) And the ancients made full use of this favorable time to go hunting in the mountains, and usually returned with a full load.

But fishing was still the major part of their economy, as it was easier and the harvest was more guaranteed. Among the 61 species of animal remains unearthed at the Hemudu Site, as many as 21 species were aquatic creatures, living in freshwater, in the sea, or at coastal river mouths. The number of these remains was huge. There were more than 2,000 tortoises, and a similar number of soft-shelled turtles (鳖类). Many ceramic cauldrons (陶罐) contained the remains of tortoises, soft-shelled turtles, mussels, fish and other aquatic creatures when unearthed. Mussel shells were found in piles, and fish bones were even found in dog dung.

However, the fishing tools excavated from the Hemudu culture were very few, except for the several bone fish darts mentioned above, and only two or three pieces of net sinkers which used to be found frequently in other prehistoric sites. Since the Hemudu ancients could already knit mats with reeds and could spin and weave about 7,000 years ago, it is reasonable to say that the weaving of fishing nets was not a problem at all. The fact that they could but did not do it indicates that there was no such need at that time. It seemed that fishing with bare hands should be the most common method used by the Hemudu ancients, and that a large number of tortoises, soft-shelled turtles, mussels, and crabs would be easily gained this way. In addition, at that time, there were many shallow lakes and swamps near the villages. The ancients could build a weir to enclose an area, drain the water, and catch the whole lot in one go. What's more, there are many cases of shooting fish with bows and arrows at home and abroad according to ethnological literature, and considering the large number of bone arrowheads excavated in the Hemudu culture, it was very likely that they were used to shooting fish.

During long fishing activities, the Hemudu ancients also had their share of luck. The village was much closer to the coast than it is now. The huge whales and sharks in the ocean sometimes came along with the tide and would be stranded on the beach when the tide was out. When villagers found them, they cut them up with tools and brought them back home for food.

VI. Rice as the Staple Food and Fish as the Main Dish

Food is the basis for human survival and development. The Hemudu ancients lived a relatively stable settled life, and had a quite good diet as far as their productivity was concerned. There was a wide variety of food: some could allay their hunger; some were high in protein; some were starchy. "Rice as the staple food and fish as the main dish", a term from *Shiji* (《史记》, *The Records of the Grand Historian*), is a good description of their dietary habits.

The economy of the Hemudu ancients mainly relied on rice farming. But activities such as fishing, hunting, gathering, and livestock rearing greatly enriched their food sources. The animals in the mountains and forests, the livestock they raised, the large number of aquatic products, the wild vegetables, fruits, and tuberous roots, as well as the mushrooms and bird eggs were all brought to the table and became their delicacies. Some could be eaten directly and presumably were eaten raw, such as water chestnuts and peach, as indicated by remains of the shells broken in half and peach kernels. However, most of the food had to be cooked, and others even had to be processed before cooking. For example, rice had to be hulled, acorns had to be rid of astringency and ground into flour, and fish had to be scaled.

The rice accumulation found in the Hemudu culture was composed mainly of rice husks and wood chips, with a very small proportion of intact rice grains. The Hemudu ancients must have hulled the rice and discarded the waste. Then how did they hull the rice? According to the ancient text *Zhouyi* (《周易》, *Book of Changes*), "cutting wood into pestles and digging the ground into a mortar to process rice" (断木为杵， 掘地为臼) was the common practice in ancient China. But further research is needed to confirm whether any mortar was dug into the ground. A number of wooden pestles were found from the Hemudu culture, one featuring a streamlined appearance with an oval-shaped head, and another with a cylindrical head, a short small wooden handle, and a hole in the middle for hand grip. The pestles were probably matched with pottery mortars or wooden mortars (木臼). The pottery mortar was shaped like a pottery basin, but larger and with a much heavier wall, and two symmetrical crown-shaped lugs in the middle of the outer wall to facilitate movement. Wooden mortars were not excavated. However, the excavation of wooden building components and wooden tools indicated that the level of carpentry work was quite advanced and that they were fully capable of making wooden mortars.

Whether the Hemudu ancients used stone grinding sticks and grinding plates to process grains needs further study, but a lot of grindstones were unearthed. Some had large flat surfaces, resembling stone grinding plates in shape. They might have been used as grinders, as grooves left from tool grinding for bone plows, bone daggers, stone axes, and stone adzes could still be felt by hand on the surface. Or they might also have been used as stone grinding plates matched with stone grinding sticks made of pebbles collected in brooks. In addition, 5 curved and concave wooden boards, 50–70 centimeters long and 40–55 centimeters wide, were found at the Tianluoshan Site, somewhat resembling dustpans, with raised edges on three sides, and the curved board roughly processed into a wavy shape. When they were first discovered, they were thought to be the head or tail of a broken canoe, but later scientists took samples from their surfaces, found large amounts of starch, and realized that they were ancient wood grinding plates for the processing of starchy foods such as rice or acorns. The thick accumulation of rice husks found next to the wooden grinding plates also suggested a close relationship between them. Matched with the grinding plate was a small, rectangular grinding board with a carved handle. Pits of acorns were often found, and it was hardly ever the case with other food and was in fact a method to remove the astringent taste of acorns. There were different ways to deal with their bitter taste. In ancient Japan, they were often buried in pits on the banks of rivers and lakes to remove the astringent taste and keep freshness. And it is thought that the Hemudu ancients did the same. Heaps and piles of fish scales were also frequently found during archeological excavations, suggesting that the Hemudu ancients also removed fish scales when cooking fish, a habit fully consistent with modern life.

The processed food was also cooked to make it sterilized and easy to digest and absorb. However, before human ancestors knew how to use fire, everything obtained from fishing and hunting was eaten raw. It was only by chance that they discovered that food cooked by fire was both easy to chew and more tasty. Therefore, they gradually began to grill some food over the fire on purpose, and it was one of the most primitive methods of cooking. Without any cooking utensils, cooking could be done by just putting or hanging the food over the fire. This method of grilling also existed in the Hemudu culture, as proved by evidences. The remains of a jumbled pile of twigs with traces of firing in the middle was found at the site, with the remains of barbecued bones and other food remnants scattered around. At another place, a half silted-up ash pit was filled with a layer of stones as a barbecue surface, on which there was a layer of ashes mixed with fish and animal bones, some blackened from the fire. It seemed that meat food from fishing and hunting, or from domestic animals was mainly grilled directly on the fire.

With the development of *si*-tillage in the Hemudu culture's rice farming, a large amount of rice was produced and rice became the main food. But how did the people cook rice? The vessel used for cooking is called a pottery *fu*. The pottery *fu* was found, with a thick layer of soot or fire smoke (熏烤) traces at the bottom and a layer of black charred stuff tightly attached to the inner bottom, discernible with the naked eye as the crust of rice, with intact grains of rice with some still intact grains. It is the most direct evidence that the Hemudu ancients used pottery the pottery *fu* to cook rice. In modern Chinese, this character is replaced by *guo* (锅, pot). However, the character *fu* still appears in many frequently used Chinese idioms, such as *po fu chen zhou* (" 破釜沉舟 " , breaking the pot and destroying the ship so as to perish the hope of a retreat), *fu di zhou xin* (" 釜底抽薪 " , removing the burning wood under the boiling pot so as to solve the problem once and for all). Yet in ancient times, the *fu* was shaped differently and made from different materials during different periods. The cooking vessel used by the Hemudu people was a type of *fu* and also one of the most important and characteristic pottery forms of the Hemudu culture.

In the Hemudu culture, the pottery *fu* was excavated in great numbers and had a wide variety of shapes. The *fu* had to be matched with three supports, which were thick rectangular pottery blocks with the top tilted slightly to one side. The cooking method of boiling was the same as today-putting the processed food material, mainly rice, fish, meat, and wild fruits, along with a sufficient amount of water into the pottery *fu*, then placing the *fu* on three supports or three stones of suitable size above firewood, and light the fire. From the analysis of the burned rice residue and potpourri stuck to the inner bottom (锅巴), the cooked rice of the Hemudu people was like "congee" (馕粥), the word meaning thick porridge (原粥烂饭) or soft rice. Meanwhile, bone remains of tortoises, soft-shelled turtles, and fish were also found in the pottery *fu*. To place the *fu* on three supports was a practice common in many areas. But the Hemudu people sometimes just picked up three stones with proper sizes and shapes to function as the supports.

Around 6,500 years ago, the ancients invented a portable pottery stove that could cook food indoors One type was shaped like a large dustpan, with an upturned opening for wood firing in the front, three stout pegs across the inner walls to hold the *fu*, and two half-ring lugs on the outer walls for hand gripping. This kind of stove had a scientifically designed structure and was easy to control the fire. Convenient and relatively safe, it was suitable for cooking on the wooden floor in a stilt house. This has also been the earliest specialized cooker found in China so far that matched with the *fu* so far. Another kind of pottery stove was shaped like a barrel, with a round or square opening for wood firing near the bottom, and this kind of stove looked like the cylinder-shaped coal ball stove still was widely used in Ningbo in the 1960s and 1970s.

The Hemudu ancients also learned a relatively advanced cooking method — steaming, evidenced by the discovery of the pottery *zeng* (甑, steamer), which suggested that they began to have higher requirements for food. The shape of the *zeng* was the same as that of the pottery basin, except that its flat bottom was pierced with many round holes, about 1 centimeter in diameter, and that there were a pair of semi-ringed lugs on the outer wall for its move. This was similar to the household steamer basket we use today. Because of the distance between the water and the steamer, the food was separated from the boiling water, and the nutrition in the food was thus preserved. The size of the holes of the *zeng* suggested that mainly wild fruits and animal meat were steamed, instead of food in small grains such as rice.

Around 6,000 years ago, perhaps influenced by the inhabitants on the northern shore of Hangzhou Bay, the Hemudu ancients began to make and use pottery tripods. The tripods were actually the combination of the pottery *fu* and three supports, which made it more portable and convenient in use. Although the pottery tripod provided a more advanced method of cooking, it was not commonly used by the Hemudu ancients, for it was found in small numbers.

The food utensils of the Hemudu culture mainly included *bo*, plates, and *dou*. They functioned differently. The *bo* for holding the staple food of rice was equivalent to the bowls nowadays, while the plates and *dou* were equivalent to the plates for dishes nowadays. Thus, the Hemudu ancients seemed to have developed a preliminary division of staple food and secondary food during this period.

The Hemudu people's staple food was undoubtedly rice, but what were the common side dishes? The "vegetarian dishes" in their diet included gourds and lotus roots, while "meat dishes" were more varied. For instance, fish, turtles and soft-shelled turtles were cooked in the pottery *fu*. All the livestock were raised for meat in the first place. And all the animals they hunted and all the livestock they raised could be their meat dishes, mainly.

The modern mind holds that since the ancients always ate nutritious wild foods, they must have had a healthy body. But this was not the case. Due to their low productivity, they were constantly doing heavy physical work on an empty stomach. Consequently, starvation, spinal deformations, diseases, and short life spans were common. Most people died before adulthood, nearly half in infancy and adolescence.

It was likely that the Hemudu ancients started making wine, judging from the discovery of other eating utensils from the Hemudu culture, including vessels like cups, *he*, *gui*, and *yu*. The cups were often used together with *he*. Both of them were discovered in small numbers. The surface of the pottery *he* was scraped and polished, and then the exterior was coated with a red layer. The vessel has two mouths on the top, a thick and short upward mouth in the front, and a larger round mouth in the back. The whole vessel was shaped like a squatting bird, with a half-ring handle linking the two mouths. Into the larger mouth, food could be put and out of the upward mouth (冲天嘴), liquid could be poured. Some believe that it was a vessel for alcoholic drink. It is reasonable, for during the Hemudu culture, rice was already a staple food, and when the left-over rice was put aside in hot weather, or the fruits collected were put into the pottery without being eaten immediately, they were likely to give off an enticing fragrance in a few days; the liquid produced perhaps was the most primitive alcoholic drink. Nowadays, in much the same way, some people put grapes in glass bottles and wait for them to ferment naturally to make wine. Unfortunately, no other instruments related to wine making have been found so far, and it remains to be proved whether the Hemudu ancients really started making alcohol. As he was finely crafted and brilliantly colored, other precious liquid food such as honey might also have been stored inside.

The most common vessels for food storage used by the Hemudu ancients were pottery basins and jars, which had a much larger capacity than cooking and eating vessels. Since they were only used for storing food, they were mostly crude and not very well formed.

Different requirements for preservation and storage were put forward, concerning the different types of food, the different methods of preservation and storage, and the different seasons when the food had to be preserved. In particular, for animal meat and aquatic food, it has not been found out whether the Hemudu ancients dried them in the sun, smoked them, or used other methods to preserve them for longer periods of time. The absence of relevant relics and remains makes it difficult to conduct research in this area. According to literature in Japanese, primitive people who lived by the sea were often the first to master the art of making salt in pottery and use salt to preserve food. It requires further evidence in the future to prove whether Hemudu people, living not far from the coast, learned salt making and whether they used salt to pickle food.

As mentioned above, the Hemudu ancients usually cooked their food by grilling, boiling, or steaming, and often served rice in bowls and vegetables on plates or in *dou*. Making distinction between staple foods and side dishes was a dietary habit basically consistent with that in modern times. Nowadays, people eat with the help of tableware like chopsticks and spoons. Then, what kind of utensils did the Hemudu ancients use about 7,000 years ago to assist themselves in eating?

As the rice eaten by the Hemudu ancients was thick porridge in the form of a paste, which had to be served and eaten with the aid of a tool, the answer might be a certain type of bone dagger. The bone dagger was one of the common objects of the Hemudu culture, made from the ribs of a large animal after they were cut in half. The front end of the bone dagger was flat, thin, and tongue-shaped, while the back end was mostly dull and neatly processed. Since bone daggers were diverse in shape, long or short, large or small, they might have served a variety of purposes, such as weaving and wefting, repairing pottery, and so on. Some of these bone daggers function as eating utensils. They were particularly fine, smooth, flat, thin, and less than 20 centimeters long, which some archeologists now simply refer to as "bone spoons".

VII. Wells

Water is the source of life, on which human production and daily life depend. The invention of the well, a most important resource of water, was of great importance. It marked the beginning of mankind's liberation from the limit of surface water in nature and was an important sign of progress in productivity. This is because wells can not only provide clean water for living, but also facilitate irrigation and pottery production. More importantly, the appearance of wells greatly expanded the space for human survival and development to areas where surface freshwater resources were scarce.

One of the earliest wooden wells in China was found at the Hemudu Site. The well, made up of over 200 wood piles and long logs, covered an area of 28 square meters, with a diameter of about 6 meters and a depth of 1.35 meters at the time. A circle of wood piles divided the well into the inside and the outside. The remains of 28 piles were found. The intervals between the piles were uneven, with several piles missing. Most piles were about 5 centimeters in diameter and were driven vertically into the earth to a depth of about 1 meter and up to 1.42 meters. 2 piles 8 centimeters in diameter were driven into the earth at 55 degrees to the horizontal, one in the north and the other in the south, facing each other. Experts of ancient architecture speculated that this circle was a fence around the well to prevent wild animals and livestock from damaging the well. The well may also have been sheltered with a pavilion, which fully indicated the ancestors' care of the well.

Within the fence were 8 horizontal logs 1.9–2.6 meters in length and 15–18 centimeters in diameter, forming an approximately square frame as the mouth of the well (井口). Six of them were forked at one end and one had a cross mortise (十字斗口) at one end. Beneath were four rows of vertical piles, fitting into the horizontal logs to form a square shaft. In each row, piles about 6 centimeters in diameter were closely placed and roughly parallel to each other, the number ranging from 21 to 40. The corner piles were thicker. The inner side of each row was lined with a round or semi-round log. The semi-round log in the north and the counterpart in the south were 17 centimeters in diameter, with an oblong mortise 1.3 centimeters wide and 1.8 centimeters long at both ends. The round logs in the east and the west had tenons at both ends. Another square frame was thus formed by the four logs connected through the tenons and mortises, which was still well preserved when unearthed.

According to the archeological data above, the well was originally a shallow pot-shaped water pit located within the settlement, naturally formed or artificially dug. During the rainy season, when the pit was filled with water, people could collect water from the outside. During the dry season, when the water level in the pit gradually dropped, people had to put stones into the pit and get water from the inside while stepping on the stones. Sometimes the water in the pit was almost depleted. To solve the problem, a shaft was dug in the middle of the pit. Four rows of small piles were driven into the center of the pit to form a square wall, and then the soil inside the rows of piles was hollowed out. To prevent the piles from tilting inwards, a frame of round or semi-round timbers connected with mortise and tenon joints was installed at the top of the piles. The 16 long round logs on the piles were likely to have formed the frame or to have been installed to reinforce the mouth of the well.

Two wells were found at the Tianluoshan Site too. One was about 1.8 meters deep, with a roughly round-cornered square top, steep walls, and a square bottom. Seven parallel planks were placed at the bottom, and a hole was cut into the wall for feet to step on when going up and down the well. The other was originally a circular pond with a deep round pit dug in the center, with a step made of a large, heavy rectangular plank and a flat stone beneath to facilitate access to water in the center during the dry season.

These two wells dated back to around 6,000 years ago, similar to the age of the wooden well at the Hemudu Site.

All the wells found in the Hemudu culture were less than 2 meters deep, indeed much shallower than the wells in the middle and lower reaches of the Yellow River, which averaged 6–7 meters in depth. So it is speculated that they were not wells but things for other uses, for the Ningbo-Shaoxing Plain was and is an area with many lakes and rivers, both in prehistoric times and in modern times, and there seemed to be no urgent need to exploit groundwater.

At first glance, this argument does seem reasonable, but on a closer analysis, it is not the case. First of all, the relatively soft 3rd and 4th cultural layers through which the wells were dug were the main underwater layers in the area. Today, the wells in the nearby countryside usually go down to the depth of no more than three or four meters, at the same altitude as that of the Hemudu culture wells. Therefore, there would be a large influx of groundwater at a depth of more than 1 meter, and those primitive wells clearly fulfilled the primary requirement for a well. Secondly, a number of pottery pot fragments were found in the wooden wells at the Hemudu Site, and on one piece a cord was threaded through its ear. So it seemed that the pot was used to draw water from the well. In addition, their uses as deep cellars for grain storing in the north could also be excluded here. In the middle and lower reaches of the Yellow River, the low water table made it difficult to reach the groundwater by digging ditches and pits. So, most of the deep prehistoric cellars were dug to store food, some even more than four or five meters deep. For example, a 5.2-meter-deep cellar in the Cishan Mountain (磁山), Wu'an County, Hebei Province, was found, with nearly 2 meters of greenish gray silt formed by grain decay at the cellar bottom beneath a layer of small pebbles and three piles of pig bones. But the low-lying lower reaches of the Yangtze River have a high water table. As groundwater often gushes out at a depth of about 1 meter in the lake and marsh areas of the plain, food storage in deep cellars is seldom adopted. So, the cellars were presumably shallower and mostly used for storing wild fruits or seeds. For example, all the storage pits found in the Hemudu culture, generally 30–40 centimeters deep, were used for storing acorns. Pits more than 1 meter deep were more likely to have functioned as wells.

The Yuyao-Cicheng Plain, where the Hemudu ancients lived, had abundant water resources from lakes and rivers. So there seemed to be no need for wells. Then why did they dig wells? The answer was related to the geological features of the plain. About 8,000 years ago, the low-lying Yuyao-Cicheng Plain was formed during the gradual sea transgression, with lakes and swamps covering most of the area. In many sites, a wide range of marine foraminifera fossils, spores of halophile Chenopodiaceaes, and remains of sharks, whales, tunas, and sea turtles were excavated in the soil layers formed during the sea transgression. The low-lying coastal location of the Yuyao-Cicheng Plain led to the first reason for making wells, namely, the rising and falling of the sea tide resulted in the high salinity of the water in the rivers and lakes. Until 1958, before the construction of the sluice gate on the Yuyao River, the high tide of seawater could reach up to the downtown of Yuyao County, and people living along the river could often catch the washed-up crabs and jellyfish. For another reason, located in the subtropical monsoon climate zone (亚热带季风气候区), catastrophic weather conditions such as heavy and concentrated precipitation often harass this area, flooding and polluting rivers and lakes. The dirty salt water was unfit for drinking. So the Hemudu ancients, with the experience accumulated during their long production practices, used natural ponds and artificially excavated water pits or wells to obtain water for daily life, which may account for why wells were invented in the coastal area.

Two of the above-mentioned wells were originally a natural or artificial pit or pond, and it seemed likely that they were dug deeper into wells. Digging a well in such a way, namely with a large open mouth and a small base, proved to cost more work and cause more inconvenience in drawing water than digging a straight well (直筒形水井). So people gradually turned to straight wells. The rainwater reserved in pits and ponds would dry up over a long period of time. By digging them deeper into wells, the phreatic water would not dry even in seasons of great drought. Therefore, wells have been in use since their invention in the Late Neolithic Period. Still, as the distribution area of the Hemudu culture was once flooded by seawater, even today the water from deep wells still has a slightly salty and bitter taste. But the water in the ponds is salt-free, as it is made up of freshwater from the rainfall in the area, and the muddy water in the ponds after rain will become clear after a period of settling. This was why ponds did not disappear after the wells appeared in the area. Till the 20th century, a great number of ponds could still be seen in the Yuyao-Cicheng Plain, but with a wider coverage and a larger volume than those in the Neolithic Age. Till the 20th century, a great number of ponds could still be seen in the Yuyao-Cixi Plain, but with a wider coverage and a larger volume than those in the Neolithic Age. In each village, there were still several ponds. Some villages were even named after the ponds.

In spite of the legends that the inventor of the well in China was the Yellow Emperor (黄帝), or Bo Yi (伯益) in the Xia Dynasty, the well was not invented overnight by any sage, but appeared along with the development of agricultural production and the stability of settled life.

The necessity and ability to dig pits, caves, and wells can be justified by the settlement and the development of agriculture in the Neolithic Period. The storage and safekeeping of agricultural harvest became the most important thing for the settlements, as agriculture developed rapidly with the invention and wide use of a large number of advanced farming tools such as the stone *si* and bone *si* in China around 7,000 years ago, which further enabled humans to settle in larger groups in the same village. Some villages began to have large cellars for crop harvest and wide, deep trenches to protect people against wild animals, enemies, and floods. For example, at the Cishan Site (磁山遗址) in Wu'an County, Hebei Province, small semi-crypt houses and several grain storage caves were found in the excavation of a total area of about 80,000 square meters, where husks and rotten ashes of millet were found, which could amount to more than 100,000 kilograms if converted into fresh grains. In these ditching and digging processes, the conditions for the invention of wells were already ripe. In the middle and lower reaches of the Yellow River, the ancients took advantage of the low water table and dug a large number of pit cellars to store grain. If they went deep enough in the digging, they would naturally encounter water coming out of the ground and might thus acquire the inspiration for the discovery and use of groundwater. In contrast, in the low-lying lower reaches of the Yangtze River, where the water table was high, the use of deep pits and caves for food storage was not as advisable as in the north. But the conditions for the emergence of wells were also present. In the case of the Hemudu culture, for example, the construction of wooden stilt houses involved digging post holes that averaged 1 meter in depth, some even reaching 1.5 meters. For another example, at the Luojiajiao Site (罗家角遗址) in Tongxiang County, Zhejiang Province, 7 of the 17 ash pits in the 4th layer were more than 1 meter deep, and one was 2.12 meters deep. Because of the high water table in the lake-marsh area, where groundwater can be seen at around 1 meter from the surface, wells were invented soon after these digging activities.

Let us imagine that about 7,000 years ago, many primitive tribes in the above-mentioned regions had already mastered the techniques necessary for well digging, thanks to the invention of handy digging tools and the experience gained from long periods of trenching and digging. In the case of the Hemudu ancients living in the coastal plain, although the surroundings were vast rivers, lakes and marshes, these waters were salty, turbid, and undrinkable as they were directly connected to the sea. So the primitive people took advantage of the high water table and dug wells to obtain clean water for domestic use.

VIII. Pioneers of Marine Culture

About 7,000 years ago, the Hemudu people became pioneers of marine culture as a result of their living environment. They settled by the vast waters of lakes, rivers, and swamps, and their life was inseparable from water. As we already know, aquatic plants and animals were their important source of food. Fishes in the coastal waters like flathead gray mullets and the *Gymnocranius*, and even those in the sea like sea turtles, whales, tunas, and sharks, were also included in their diet. In shallow waters, people could catch fish and mussels without watercraft, but in deeper waters or coastal areas, they had to rely on watercraft. The emergence of oars not only promoted the rapid development of fishing but also expanded their scope of activities and catalyzed their cultural exchange with the neighboring people. The surging Qiantang River and the turbulent Hangzhou Bay did not hinder the exchange between the two neighboring cultures — the Hemudu culture and the Majiabang culture, in which watercraft was instrumental. The settlement sites found in the Zhoushan Islands showed that the Hemudu ancients not only traveled freely in inland rivers and lakes, but also mastered navigation techniques to cross shallow seas.

So far, more than 20 wooden oars from the Hemudu culture have been found. The oars were made from whole pieces of hardwood. The handles, mostly rounded, with a few square exceptions, were of medium thickness for hand grip. The top of the oar was shaped into an inverted triangle to facilitate the hand grip when rowing. The finely crafted flat willow-shaped blades were gradually thinned from the upper to the lower part. Some of the blades had a rounded square tip while others a pointed one, similar in shape to the wood oars used on small boats in the rural areas south of the lower reaches of the Yangtze River nowadays. Two oars unearthed were especially fine. One was in deep red when excavated, made of hardwood, the upper part of its handle slightly mutilated. The link between the handle and the blade was carved with geometric patterns composed of straight and diagonal lines, embodying esthetic values aside from the practical ones. The other oar had a blade, and its upper part was entwined with plant fibres. In the Hemudu culture, skills for making wood oars were well developed. With thin and light blades, the oars were light and practical in use.

Generally speaking, boats were invented before oars. There must have been a boat if there was an oar. According to ethnographic literature, the method of making a canoe, the earliest boat, was relatively simple. First, the selected thick log was cut in half or cut flat on one side. Then the middle part of the plane was grilled with fire, and simultaneously a cabin was carved out with adzes and chisels. By burning and digging, the cabin was gradually widened and deepened, and then a little trimming was done to the canoe. Since the Hemudu ancients were able to use stone tools to make woodwork and advanced mortise-and-tenon wood components, using stone adzes, stone chisels, and fire to make canoes was not a difficult task. Yet so far no finished canoes or other forms of boats have been found in the Hemudu culture, which is related to the fact that the excavation sites were in the living areas or in the rice fields, rather than in the "docks" where the boats were moored. Fortunately, in 2013, an unfinished canoe blank was found at the Tianluoshan Site, nearly 4 meters long and 0.6 meters wide at the widest point of the tail, with one side cut flat and a shallow, irregular pit cut near the top of the tree. Complete canoes can be seen at other prehistoric sites in Zhejiang Province. For example, the around 8,000-year-old canoe found at the Kuahuqiao Site in Xiaoshan District, was 5.6 meters long and 0.52 meters wide, with a narrow, upturned prow. The hull was smoothly crafted, with a number of black scorched places on the inside, which evidenced the processing of the hull with the help of fire. At the Maoshan Site (茅山遗址) in Yuhang District, an around 5,000-year-old canoe was also found, hewn from a whole section of giant wood, with only slight damage in several parts. It was 7.35 meters long, 0.45 meters wide at its widest point, and about 0.23 meters deep, with a pointed head and a square tail. Another precious piece of evidence is that the Hemudu ancients, skilled in the art of pottery molding, left us several pieces of artwork based on the canoes of the time. One of them was shaped like a rectangular tank, slightly mutilated on one side, 8.7 centimeters long, 2.6 centimeters wide, and 3 centimeters high, obviously a model of a rectangular canoe with a square head. Another was the model of a shuttle-shaped canoe with pointed ends. It was shaped like a half-moon in side view and a shuttle in top view, hollowed out in the middle, slightly pointed and upturned at both ends, with a small flat ear perforated under the head for threading the cable. The third, with a pointed head and a rounded tail, and with a small cylinder on the pointed end for tying the cable, was a different type. There seemed to be various shapes of canoes at the time.

It took a long time to invent the boats and oars. The earliest boats probably imitated the natural driftwood, only large logs that kept their "passengers" from sinking. Later, flat-bottomed canoes with space for people to move around inside them emerged. The ancient Chinese books *Shiben* (《世本》) and *Zhouyi* suggest that the invention of ancient rafts and boats was inspired by the natural phenomenon of falling leaves and trees floating in water, and that the boat was developed from the raft, which was a watercraft made of a certain number of bamboos or logs. As it was easy to obtain and process bamboos and logs, rafts could have been made during the Early or Middle Neolithic Period. For example, at the Nanhu Lake (南湖) in Yuhang District the bamboo raft of the Liangzhu culture was found lying flat in the mud of the river and was relatively well preserved, being 2.8 meters long and 0.6 meters wide and made of five thick bamboo strips knitted together. Rafts can be propelled by a tree branch or a bamboo pole in shallow waters, or by an oar in offshore waters. Even today, bamboo and wood rafts can still be seen in some mountainous rivers and streams from time to time. From the superior carpentry techniques reflected in the wooden oars, canoes, ropes, and wood components unearthed at the Hemudu Site, it was possible that the

Hemudu people used rafts, although no rafts have been discovered so far.

Boats will not move forward or turn around without oars. At first, perhaps, the boat was paddled with the bare hands, then in some shallow water areas it was propelled with sticks and bamboo poles. In deeper waters, however, sticks and bamboo poles were not able to reach the river bed and were used for paddling only. Later, the more efficient thin-bladed oars (薄叶桨) appeared. The boats and oars used by the Hemudu ancients would be of this advanced type.

The fact that some of the Hemudu ancients crossed the sea about 6,000 years ago and settled in the Zhoushan Islands tells us that the ancients had already had some navigational skills. Canoes and bamboo rafts are reliable in inland rivers and lakes with calm wind and water flow. But once in the wavy sea, canoes will capsize easily when the wind is strong and the waves are high. It is now common practice for indigenous people living on islands off the Pacific coast to tie a wooden frame to one or both sides of a canoe to make an outrigger canoe that can ride the waves at sea. This simple facility is very practical and can withstand the wind and waves well in the sea to keep the canoe balanced, thus ensuring the safety of navigation at sea. When some of the Hemudu ancients wanted to move to the Zhoushan Islands, they probably traveled in such outrigger canoes.

From canoes and rafts to boats, people's sphere of activity expanded, barriers to transport were cleared away, and the first people gained more and more freedom on the waters.

IX. Knitting and Weaving

Clothing, a basic human need, is as important as eating. It can fulfill both practical functions and aesthetic functions, providing the body with warmth, dignity, and decoration. Thus, weaving has been an important handicraft in all societies. Since as early as about 18,000 years ago, Peking Men at the Zhoukoudian Site（周口店遗址）had already made bone needles to sew "clothes" made out of animal furs or leaves during the Late Paleolithic. However, though warm in winter, furs were a bit uncomfortable in hot summer. Leaf clothing felt cooler in summer, but leaves would dry up soon and fall off in pieces. Therefore, during the Neolithic Period, primitive textile skills（原始纺织技术）emerged. People learned to make use of wild plant fibers such as hemp, degumming the fibers, twisting them into threads, and finally weaving threads into cloth.

However, knitting had existed long before the advent of primitive weaving. It was the original form of weaving. Knitting has continued to flourish in the service of mankind for millions of years, producing items like straw hats, mats, ropes, baskets, nets, and wickets. In our daily life, we still often come into contact with knitted products. Archeological findings show that the Hemudu ancients' knitting craft had already been well developed and played an important part in their life.

The Hemudu ancients mainly knitted reeds into mats and twisted plant fibers into ropes. During archeological excavations, more than a hundred pieces of reed mats were found near houses or at the bottom of ash pits, their size ranging from the coverage of a palm to more than 1 square meter. When first unearthed, the reed mats were well preserved, bright yellow in color, and clear in texture. But just like the rice, they became discolored, dried, and cracked soon after excavation. The mats were made from reeds grown in the local lakes and swamps. With the leaves and roots removed, the reed stalks were cut into long thin strips of 0.4 to 0.5 centimeters in width, most of which were of the same thickness. Usually, 2 strips were grouped into a strand, or 4–6 strips into a strand. Then the strands were arranged into vertical warps and horizontal wefts, and woven into mats with a twill or herringbone pattern (斜纹或人字纹), like the patterns of the fabric texture today. The clear warps and wefts were evenly spaced into a smooth surface with simple patterns, fully showing the skillfulness of the knitter. At first sight, you might think these are bamboo summer sleeping mats used by the farmers nearby.

These reed mats were used for a wide range of purposes. During the construction of a house, they could be used to support thatched roofs on the rafters and to separate rooms; some of the neatly trimmed strips were woven into sitting and sleeping utensils; and some were found at the bottom of the ash pits as bedding for the cellar. During the excavations at the Tianluoshan Site, the reed mats were often found at the bottom of the cellar or on the ground, usually covered with acorns or water chestnuts. It seems more likely that they were used as bedding for storing such food. Another use of reed mats was found at the Tongjia'ao Site, Cixi County, where the roadbed was reinforced with dense, thick reed stalks and woven reed mats between the piles.

Apart from reed, other materials such as twigs of the chaste tree, rattan strips, and bamboo were used for knitting, since they grew in abundance in the surrounding mountains. For example, one of the wooden cylinders unearthed was reinforced with rattan strips at both ends to prevent cracks. Such techniques made these beautiful wood objects still well-formed even after being buried underground for thousands of years. Another wooden cylinder was painted with black lacquer, and traces of being banded with rattan strips at the two ends are still discernible. Rattan was also used to bind the wooden handle to the bone *si* tightly to make them handier in use. Moreover, whole bundles of rattan were found during the archeological excavations. Clearly, they were prepared on purpose to be used as spare rattan for weaving or repairing.

Rope making is also a kind of knitting. When primitive humans were engaged in production activities, they accumulated some knowledge of fibers from wild plants such as kudzu and hemp, and began to twist them into ropes. Several sections of rope of the Hemudu culture with different thickness were found. First, plant fibers were rolled into small strands, and then 2 or 3 strands were rolled into a rope. The thickest one was about 2 centimeters in diameter and made of two strands, each 8–10 millimeters in diameter and consisting of at least 14 fibers of hemp. The thinnest was only about 0.2 centimeters in diameter and probably made of several strands of tough grasses. Two other ropes, 1.5 centimeters in diameter, were made of three strands of fibers. The appearance of these ropes showed no difference from that of hand-made ropes today.

The ropes had various functions. A section of the rope was still worn on the ear of a pottery jar when it was unearthed, and some were left in the square hole of a plowshare (骨耜方銎) or in the hole of a pottery *fu*, which showed that in addition to being used for tying, ropes were also used on pottery jars to draw water. In addition, they were also used in house building to bind different building components together and reinforce them. The mortise and tenon technique was already used in the houses of the Hemudu culture, but in most places components were still bound with ropes. If the Hemudu people also used to "keep records by tying knots" like some ethnic minorities in China, ropes could have play another role in the Hemudu culture.

The production of textile includes both "spinning" and "weaving". In a broad sense, the rope and the reed mat mentioned earlier were the products of primitive "spinning" and "weaving", respectively. Later, people regarded spinning and weaving as a whole and gave both activities the only name "weaving". Although no textiles have been found so far, woven patterns were common on the excavated objects, mainly on bone objects such as bone hairpins (骨笄) and daggers. More importantly, many valuable textile tools have been unearthed, with a wide variety, mainly spinning tools, weaving tools, and sewing tools.

Spinning tools, mainly pottery spindle whorls for twisting threads, have been excavated in large numbers. There were also some stone or wood ones. The hand-made pottery spindle whorls were regularly shaped, mainly taking the form of a flat disc and having a rectangular longitudinal section, with some exceptions I-shaped (工字形的) or trapezoidal. The spindle whorls were mainly plain on the surface, but a few were carved and poked with a variety of patterns, which were not only for esthetic purposes, but also useful for judging the rotation direction and speed of the spindle whorl. In the late period, the number of pottery spindle whorls declined and finely polished stone ones appeared, most of which were made of dark red pyrophyllite (暗红色叶蜡石), but a very few of fluorite. Spindle whorls were often found in women's tombs during the Neolithic Period as burial objects, but rarely in men's. This proved women's status as the inventors and workers of weaving. In the middle of the whorl was a round hole for a small wood stick to be inserted. Many sticks with rounded tips were found in the Hemudu culture, presumably used on spindle whorls. When spinning, the whorl was first spun with external force to stretch and twist fibers into yarn, and the yarn was wrapped around a wood spindle stick ready for weaving. Archeologists found two small thread balls at the Tianluoshan Site. The thickness of the thread was about 2 millimeters, almost the same as the fine thread used to sew clothes today, reflecting the advanced development of the textile craft at that time.

The step next to spinning was weaving. The primitive weaving method was extremely simple, that is, wrapping one end of the warp thread around the waist and fixing the other end to a pole or pile, threading the "weft" back and forth horizontally with a spindle stick repeatedly, and beating-up the weft to make the fabric tight with a knife or a dagger, which is called a "beater", equivalent to the later "reed". The ancient Chinese book *Huainanzi* (《 淮

南子》) has described a similar weaving procedure, which roughly reflects the craft of the Hemudu culture as well. Some of China's peoples and some small workshops also used these textile tools in the near past. The Tibetan Monba people and Lhoba people used wooden beaters to beat-up weft, and the weft beater of the Li people in Hainan were either wooden or bamboo, all basically similar in appearance.

A large number of hardwood rods (木磨棒) of different sizes with round cross-sections were found in the Hemudu culture, some with one end pointed and the other flattened or rounded, some with both ends pointed, and some tenoned at one end or both ends. Most of these rods were the warp beams (定经杆), heddle shafts (综杆), hank bars (绞纱棒), and warp-tying logs on a primitive loom (原始织机). The shuttle was one of the weaving tools and played an important role in guiding the wefts through the warps. Two Hemudu culture shuttles made of antlers were excavated. One had a sharpened shuttle blade, with a circular ridge carved out at the other end, and the two rectangular holes cut in the front of the shuttle were connected with the rectangular groove cut in the back. The other had a smoothly polished and slightly curved body, with a barb in the middle and a blunt ridge. The weft beater, with a thick back and a thin blade, was generally made of hardwood and sometimes animal ribs. It was long and slender, and have two sizes. The cloth beam was an important part of the primitive loom. The length of the beam was equal to the width of a person's waist, and the notches or grooves at its ends were for the attachment of a belt to prevent the beam from turning. Flat and long wooden toothed tools, with serrated teeth on one side, were probably used for combing and fixing warp yarns. The shapes of the teeth were triangular, trapezoidal, or comb-like. Based on these excavated weaving tools and other ethnographic data, experts speculate that the Hemudu ancients had already invented a primitive horizontal loom attached to the weaver's waist, called the waist loom. The loom was simple to operate. One end of the warp threads was usually tied to a wood pile driven in the ground, the other end tied to a cloth beam in front of the weaver's waist. The weaver sat on the ground, with both legs stretched out on either side of the loom, and then wove the cloth by threading wefts through warps. The operation process of the loom was: to draw the weft with a knife, strike the weft with the knife, divide the heddle with the knife, and repeat the whole process. Each time the shuttle was used to guide the weft, and the odd and even numbered warp threads alternated as the ground warp and the face warp. Finally, the fabric was interwoven into the cloth with the repetition of the practice.

What did the primitive loom of the Hemudu culture look like? When a precious bronze container for shells from the Han Dynasty was unearthed at the Shizhaishan Site (石寨山遗址) in Jinning District, Yunnan Province, the carvings on its lid caught much attention: the statue of a female slave master overseeing a circle of women weavers seated in front of their looms in various forms, either holding threads with both hands, weaving with a shuttle, beating weft with a wooden beater, or combing warp yarns, all vividly portrayed. The looms they used were perch looms. The physical entities of this ancient loom can still be found today in the life of some ethnic minority groups, including areas of the Liangshan Yi people in Sichuan Province, the Li people in Hainan Province, the Jingpo, Drung, Dai, Naxi, Hani, Va, Pumi, Miao, Lahu in Yunnan Province. And they have been the major reference for the restoration of the primitive loom of the Hemudu culture.

Sewing tools mainly include bone needles, small bone awls, and small stone adzes. The bone needles were large in number, varied in length, and similar in size to the modern steel needles used for sewing sacks. They were finely ground, and the needle-eyes at the back end were only about 1 millimeter in diameter. This required the sewing thread to be of high quality, not only thin but also soft and tough, indicating the developed textile craft at that time. The thickness of the two balls of thread found in the fish bone pit at the Tianluoshan Site was about the diameter of a rice grain, and just thin enough to pass through the eyelet of a bone needle. Bone awls were made from animal limb bones that were cut open and finely ground, generally long and slender, with sharp edges. A small number of particularly finely honed small stone adzes were unearthed from the Hemudu culture. And they were polished so that people could grip it in hand to cut hides or textiles.

Although no silk fabrics have been found so far in the Hemudu culture, the image of the silkworm had already appeared. There were two cap-shaped ivory vessels, one of which was carved with two bands of string pattern on the outer wall, interspersed with diagonal woven patterns, with a band of silkworm-shaped design below; the other was carved with a broad band of diagonal woven pattern and a band of silkworm-like (incomplete) design on the outer wall. Although the image of the silkworm alone is not sufficient to suggest that silk had already been produced, many artifacts related to weaving have been found in the Hemudu culture, such as thick and thin ropes, reed mats, bone daggers with woven patterns, and many more tools for sewing and weaving. Most importantly, the discovery of two balls of fine thread at the Tianluoshan Site conveys to us the information about their primitive weaving. The analysis of the excavated production tools, combined with the ethnographic data and the relevant records in the ancient texts, convince us of the existence of the textile craft in the Hemudu culture. Not only did weaving exist at that time, but many of the processes were in line with scientific principles.

X. Handicrafts

Objects made of stone, bone, ivory, wood, pottery, and lacquer have all been excavated in the sites of Hemudu culture. And their processing aroused a lot of interest.

Generally speaking, the Neolithic people mainly used stone tools in their production. However, the Hemudu culture was characterized by the wide use of bone tools in all fields of production and life. And its large number and variety overshadowed all other kinds of tools. Among the over 6,000 cultural relics excavated at the Hemudu Site, about 3,000 pieces were bone tools, more than the sum of other cultural relics such as stone, pottery, and wood objects. It was really a "bone tool world" in the Stone Age.

There are more than 20 types of bone tools from the Hemudu culture, including plows, arrowheads, whistles, awls, fish darts, pyramid cones, needles, tubular needles, daggers, rods, handles, chisels, hairpins, shuttles, bird-shaped tools (butterfly shaped tools), boot-shaped tools, tooth ornaments, horn ornaments, and so on. The dazzling array of bone tools was used for a wide range of purposes, including agriculture, hunting, fishing, weaving, sewing, and decoration. The bone *si* was used for digging and plowing soil, building ridges in the fields, eradicating reeds and weeds, and processing animal hides; bone whistles (骨哨) and fish darts were used for fishing and hunting; bone needles, bone awls, and horn shuttles were used for weaving and sewing. Some bone tools had to be used in conjunction with other tools, such as bone handles, which only worked when they were fitted to stone axes or adzes. There were many kinds of decorative objects made of bone, tooth, and horn, such as chest ornaments, head ornaments, neck ornaments, and ear ornaments. Some bone tools had multiple uses, such as bone daggers, which could be used as weft beater for weaving, eating utensils, scraping tools for pottery making, or excellent decorative objects after being holed and carved with delicate patterns.

The frequent hunting activities of the Hemudu ancients brought rich harvest, providing them with an abundant source of meat and a constant supply of raw materials for bone tools. The production methods could be divided into two categories: simple processing and complex processing. For the first type, the ancients made full use of the original shape of animal bones cleverly, adapting the shapes to their needs, with as little processing as possible. For example, the scapulae of large mammals were narrow at the top and wide at the bottom, with a shape close to that of a shovel, which could be made into a bone plowshare after slight modifications; the ribs were wide and long, and could be made into bone daggers by just cutting them in half; the long end of the ulna was sharpened into a double-sided edge, which could be a bone chisel; the horns of deer and elks were forked, and could be made into handles after a little processing; the hollow bones of bird limbs could be made into bone whistles by intercepting the middle section; the sharp teeth of water deer, wild boars, tigers, and bear could be drilled and used as ornaments.

Another type required several complex processes. The hard, thick tubular bones of large- and medium-sized animals were processed to make a variety of bone tools, for example, the bone needle. The tubular bone was broken into long, thin strips of proper length, and a small hole was drilled with a sharp instrument such as a shark's teeth, as the needle-eye for threading. It was then finely rounded and polished on a grindstone. From the making of a bone needle, we can see how difficult and complex it was to make bone objects. So it is easy to understand why most of the bone objects were processed at key parts only, relying on the natural form of the bone as much as possible.

Pottery was an everyday necessity for cooking, eating, drawing water, and storing in prehistoric people's life. But for its fragility, it had to be continuously produced to replenish wear and tear and to meet people's needs. The invention of pottery can be traced back to the Early Neolithic Period.

At first, people used baskets coated with clay to hold water. For accidental reasons, the baskets burned, but the clay became hard and retained the shape of the basket. Thus, pottery was invented. Among the Early Neolithic pottery excavated from the Xianrendong Site in Jiangxi Province, the basket pattern marks were often seen inside the vessels. The mold was woven with twigs and pasted with clay, and while the basket mold was burned off after firing, the hardened clay retained the basket shape. This most primitive "molding method" of pottery making has had a history of more than 10,000 years, and has been passed on in settlements of the Va people in Cangyuan Va Autonomous County（沧源佤族自治县）, Yunnan Province, and some people in Taiwan Province, in modern times. Later, people went through a transitional stage of pottery making. After the initial molding, they removed the basket from the greenware and continued to adjust the shape by hand. Finally, people started shaping pottery directly without using the basket mold. And the materials, shapes, techniques, and decorations of pottery continued to improve and finally varied from era to era and region to region. These changes in pottery were more pronounced than those in vessels of other materials. So archeologists tend to date and analyze cultural landscapes according to the texture, decoration, shape, and craft of the excavated pottery.

The number of Hemudu culture pottery ware is astonishing, with hundreds of thousands of pieces unearthed at the Hemudu Site alone, among which more than 1,000 were complete or could be restored. This is very rare among other prehistoric sites. Pottery was invented about 10,000 years ago. And till the Hemudu culture about 7,000 years ago, pottery making craft had become more mature and unique after thousands of years of development. The clay was locally sourced, but not just any clay could be used to make pottery. After a long period of practice, the Hemudu people finally chose sericite clay, which has low iron content, as the raw materials. In order to reduce shrinkage and cracking during the drying and firing, and to improve the heat resistance of the pottery, they mixed the clay with pre-charred plant stems, leaves, and rice grains. As a result of the presence of large quantities of charred plants, which failed to fully oxidize in the firing, the finished pottery was black, with even blacker inner walls. So, they are called "charcoal-tempered black pottery". In addition to mixing charcoal particles in the clay, there were also practices of mixing sand in the clay, which was sand-tempered pottery. At a later stage, there was a relatively pure product without the mixing of other materials, called clay pottery.

The Hemudu culture pottery was all directly handmade, and later the slow-wheel trimming technique (慢轮修整技术) was developed. For a small vessel, it was generally shaped by hand and then further pasted on the outside. It looked crude, and some of the clay would fall off after firing, making it look worse. For most pottery, first, long strips of clay was rolled before hand, stacked with one circle on top of the other, and smoothed to create the desired shape. The accessories, such as handles, ears, and spouts, were made beforehand, placed on the body when the body was already shaped but not yet dried, and finally reinforced with wet clay around the joints. This process can be seen clearly through the traces on the excavated vessel fragments.

After the greenware was shaped into the desired form, the inner wall was held in place by the palm or another object, while the outer wall was reinforced through being tapped with a clay paddle, in order to make the rolls of clay sticking closely to each other. The mushroom-shaped clay paddle was wrapped with ropes before use. There were also paddles engraved with a cord pattern on the flat face. Today, in Yunnan Province, the Va people in Ximeng Va Autonomous County (西盟佤族自治县) and the Dai people in Jinghong County often use pebbles as a holder during the patting. The Hemudu people might have done that too. After the reinforcement was scraping and polishing, in order to make the surface of the vessel smooth and dense, and to conceal the marks left in shaping and patting. Tools made of long, narrow bamboo or wood pieces with a sloping edge, shaped like a dagger, or with a semi-circular edge, were essential for the scraping of the pottery surface or the trimming of the rim. Bone daggers might also have been included in the scraping tools for Hemudu culture pottery.

After being reinforced and adjusted, the greenware had to be decorated with patterns before it dried. The Hemudu people emphasized the practical function of pottery decoration. Pottery ware was decorated with different patterns according to their different uses, materials, and parts to be decorated. As people then used to sit on the ground, most decorations were in the part that people could see when sitting on the ground, such as the mouth and neck, and shoulder of the pottery, or in the part that was not easily worn. The main methods of decoration were incising, embossing, stamping, and pressing. The most common patterns included the cord pattern and the geometric pattern, followed by the string pattern, the grain pattern, the shell-edge pattern, the wave pattern, the serrated pattern, the ring pattern, comb-pricked dots pattern, and the grass leaf pattern. Whether the decorative pattern was simple or complicated, the combination was neat and orderly, with strong local features. The cord pattern was commonly patted on the lower abdomen and the bottom of the pottery *fu* with clay paddles, and functioned in several ways. Originally, the cord pattern on the pottery surface was caused in the process of pressing cord-wrapped paddles against the pottery wall for reinforcement, but later it was found that the fine and regular pattern could decorate the vessel. In addition, with the cord pattern, the vessel would have an uneven surface, which could increase the heat absorption rate, shorten the cooking time, and make the pottery less likely to break from abrupt heating or cooling in the cooking process. In fact, another often overlooked role of the cord pattern was that this pattern on the bottom of the pottery *fu* could increase the friction between the vessel and its supports, and prevent it from sliding and shaking, which would often happen when the bottom was a bare surface. The fine lines, strings, waves, circles, or punctures on pottery were made with bone (horn) or wooden cones. The pointed tip of the cone was finely grounded, but the rest parts were only roughly scraped smooth for grip. A considerable number of bone cones were made from antlers and animal bones, with blunted edge parts. For example, one wood cone with a round girdled handle and a small pointed tip was excavated. As for the shell-tooth pattern, it was embossed with the edge of the shell, and some circle patterns were made with slightly processed bird limbs or reed stalks. On some handles or ridges attached to the vessels, patterns were also made by hand through kneading and pressing. The geometric patterns of straight lines, vertical lines, diagonal lines, arcs, circles, and dots were the second most decoration only next to the cord pattern, mostly found on the rim and shoulders of everyday vessels, but rarely found on jars or spindle whorls. As for the grass leaf pattern, the leaves and stems of plants were often arranged into a triangle, with arcs or circles in the middle. A number of such patterns were connected into a chain, mostly carved on the rim of pots and plates, and occasionally on the rim of *fu*.

The exterior of storage ware such as jars, basins, plates, and single handle *bo* was further rubbed with a water-dipped tool and polished to make the surface dense and shiny. Another effect of such practice was that a layer of fine slurry was formed on the surface, and the proportion of clay in the composition of the surface was increased. After being fired, the inner pottery was black in color, but the surface showed a muddy gray or light brown color. Later, "slip" was used in pottery crafting. First, a mixture of water and clay high in iron was applied to the surface; then, the ware was fired in perfect oxidation to produce a bright red coating of the pottery product. It was in this process of surface treating that the new craft of painted pottery emerged. The painted pottery of the Hemudu culture was made by applying a thick layer of fine gray slip to the outside of the greenware, polishing it, and finally painting black images on it. The finished pottery product had a clear picture and a "glazed" surface. But it differed from the painted pottery of the Yangshao culture (仰韶文化) and the Kuahuqiao culture (跨湖桥文化) for its regional and periodical characteristics. Unfortunately, only very few fragments of painted pottery were excavated, and no complete form has been found. The information available suggests that they are fragments of jars.

Generally speaking, a kiln is always necessary for firing pottery, but no kiln has been found in the Hemudu culture so far. The reason might be that the primitive pottery making techniques did not involve the use of kilns. For example, the Va people in Yunnan Province first preheat the pottery greenware on charcoal fire, light the pile of wood on it with the pottery buried in, and finally let the ashes cool naturally. Thus, pottery is fired without any special kiln. For another instance, the Dai people in Yunnan Province lay a kiln bed on the ground with branches and pieces of wood, put the preheated greenware on the kiln floor while they are still hot, wrap them with firewood and straw on top and around, spread a layer of mud on the woodpile to seal everything in, and finally set fire to it. The thin layer of mud functioned as a primitive kiln. The Hemudu ancients might have done the same. When the firing was done, the "kiln" was opened and the pottery taken out. The early pottery often had thick walls, loose texture, low hardness, and a high water absorption rate, and the color was not even either, with mottled patches of red, black, and grey on the ware. This was mainly because it was difficult to control the firing environment in the simple and poorly sealed kiln, and the firing temperature was limited, generally between 800 ℃ and 850 ℃, yet never exceeding 900 ℃.

In the late stage of the Hemudu culture, sand-tempered pottery and clay pottery were made and used for different purposes. Cooking vessels were mostly made of hard, high-temperature resistant sandy clay pottery, while storage vessels were made of clay pottery. At that time, some people were already specialized in the production of pottery to meet the demand for pottery. It was likely that the Hemudu ancients then also built some fixed kilns and were able to produce pottery of different colors by controlling the oxidative and reductive atmosphere during firing by means of kiln sealing choices. To be specific, a half-buried kiln might have been dug on a high place, with dry wood at the bottom, pottery stacked in the middle, covered with wood and clay on top, a chimney and a fire door, both of which could be sealed when necessary.

The stone artifacts of the Hemudu culture are generally small, mostly

5–7 centimeters in height, with the largest being over 10 centimeters high. The surface of the ware was often left with various processing marks, and very few were polished throughout. The main types of stone tools, according to their use, were small carpentry tools such as axes, adzes, and chisels, sharpening tools, a few stone spindle whorls, stone knives, stone net sinkers, and human ornament jade of different shapes such as *jue*, *huang*, tubes, and beads.

As for the raw materials for the stone tools the earlier stone axes, stone adzes, stone chisels, and other carpentry tools were mostly made of black or gray flint or dark-gray siliceous rock, which have a high toughness, following the tradition of material selection from the Paleolithic Period. Such rock is characterized by its hardness, around 7 on a Mohs scale, comparable to that of steel today. When we scratch the stone tool against glass even lightly, a deep trace can be made without any damage to the stone tool. However, the shortcomings were also obvious: first, it was difficult to sharpen the edge of such stone tools; second, they was likely to crack when meeting a harder object. Therefore, the early stone tools of the Hemudu culture were only carefully sharpened on the edges, with the rest parts roughly processed. Since about 6,000 years ago, the stone materials they chose had been changed to mudstone and tuff, of less hardness, in greenish-gray, gray, or off-white color. The sharpening was relatively easy so that the whole vessel was finely polished and no traces of processing were left on the surface.

The stone spindle whorl was made of dark red pyrophyllite and grayish (or slightly greenish) fluorite. Pyrophyllite has a low hardness and a brittle texture, and thus were relatively easy to grind. In Yinzhou District, not far from the Hemudu Site, there used to be mines of pyrophyllite. Fluorite, also known as fluorspar, is of medium hardness and relatively brittle. It is abundant in the southern Siming Mountains. In addition to being used to make stone spindle whorls, fluorite was also used in a large number of decorative objects such as *jue*, *huang*, tubes, beads, and stone pellets. Among the decorative items, there were also a small number of jade pieces of lower quality. The composition of them has not been identified.

The grindstones and stone balls were reddish fine-grained quartz sandstone pieces and well-rounded pebbles. They could be found almost everywhere in creeks nearby, and could be made use of with no further processing.

The procedure of stone tool making can be restored according to traces left on the stone tools. First, the stone was quarried from the nearby hills, a rough shape was created after initial chipping, the various parts were refined, and finally the edges were carefully sharpened. The making of blanks and the fine processing of blanks involved the use of hammerstones, which were in fact discarded stone tools. Some of the discarded stone axes were scarred all over their surfaces from striking, indicating their function as hammerstones. After the final sharpening process on the grindstone, the tool would have a very sharp edge.

In addition to ground stone tools, there were also many small chipped stone tools in the Hemudu culture, all of which were made of flint, a tough and hard material. Flint, easy to chip and difficult to grind, was a common material used by primitive people in the Paleolithic Period. Most of the stone tools of the Hemudu culture were used directly after being chipped from large stone blocks as scrapers (削骨器), pointed tools (尖状器), and cutters, evidenced by traces of use on their edges. The discovery of these small flint stone tools provides an important clue to the origin of the Hemudu culture.

Wooden tools were among the earliest tools to be used by man. However, as wooden tools were more likely to decay and could rarely be preserved underground for decades or centuries, let alone for thousands of years, only a limited number of wooden tools have been unearthed.

The unique underground environment of the Yuyao-Cicheng Plain has allowed for the preservation of a large number of organic artifacts. Benefited from these favorable conditions, a large number of wooden objects of the Hemudu culture were unearthed, including *si*, shovels, pestles, knives, daggers, mallets, spades, hoes, spears, bowls, cylinders, *dou*, small wooden sticks, handles, spindle whorls, gyroscopes, and bird-shaped (butterfly-shaped) artifacts. Many of these objects were rarely or never seen in the past. So it is difficult to name them other than by their shapes, let alone to understand their purposes.

The wooden *si*, made after the shape of the bone *si* and serving the same purposes, played an important role in the rice farming. The wooden shovel looked similar to the modern shovel, though the handle was shorter, and the blade much wider than that of the wooden *si*; its use was unclear. The wooden pestles had either a spherical head with a long handle or a long cylindrical head with a short handle, used together with the mortar to husk rice and process other foods. The wooden handle could be combined with a stone ax, a stone adze, or a bone *si* to form a composite tool. The spindle whorl was a textile tool, and knives and daggers were sometimes used in weaving to tighten weft yarns. The wooden spear was a very effective stabbing weapon in hunting. The two pointed hardwood sticks were used in agriculture for dibbling and sowing seeds, as well as for digging up roots and peeling stems when collecting wild plants. The wooden mallet was a processing tool with two parts, the head and the handle. Wooden bowls and *dou* were household utensils. Yet the use of the wooden cylinders and the bird-shaped artifacts is unknown.

Most of the materials used for wooden tools were mulberry trees, which have a loose texture, and trees like Chinese pistaches, Chinese juniper, Western soapberry, and Maclura trees, and ginkgoes were also favored for they were easy to work with, moisture-resistant, and decay-resistant, each with beautiful grain. Most of the wooden tools were made by cutting, chopping, gouging, and grinding, all of which could not be done without tools such as stone axes, stone adzes, and grindstones. For some production tools, there was a special process of fire-hardening at the end. It is highly likely that the fire marks on the tips of the Hemudu people's sticks were formed because of this. People had mastered the technique of fire hardening from very early times, as evidenced by an Early Paleolithic wooden spearhead made of yew with its tip hardened by fire, unearthed in England. Similar examples can also be found among the indigenous peoples in Oceania, where the tips of wooden spears and sticks used for digging were hardened by fire.

XI. Aesthetics

The pursuit of beauty is human nature. As early as in the Paleolithic Period, humans started bedecking themselves. Some people associated the color red with blood, life, and soul; some others drilled shells and hung the string of shells around the neck or on the chest, as a primitive "necklace". As productivity increased, humans had more time and energy to discover and create beauty. The Hemudu people of about 7,000 years ago were no exception. They liked to make themselves look beautiful.

Legend has it that the Yue people in Ningbo cut their hair and wore tattoos during the Shang and Zhou Dynasties. However, the Hemudu ancients neither cut off their hair, nor wore it down. Instead, they used bone hairpins to bind it. Most hairpins were made of thick bones, some of ivory, and could be classified roughly into two types according to their shapes: one was a long and thin strip; the other was a strip with a thin front and a wide end. The back half of pins were mostly carved with a combination of the string pattern, the diagonal pattern, or the woven pattern, which suggested the owner's fondness for them. After binding their hair, they wore other ornaments such as bird feathers in their hair, as evidenced by the excavation of many small pottery figures of human heads with rows of small round holes at the top of the head, which presumably have been decorated with feathers and other ornaments. The Siming Mountains in the south are rich in fluorite, a translucent crystal that shimmers in the sunlight with a light green color. The Hemudu ancients regarded it as beautiful jade (美玉) and made it into body ornaments of different shapes, such as *jue*, *huang*, tubes, beads, and rings. The *jue* had the shape of a round ring with a small opening, and was worn in the same way as today's earrings, by first making a hole in the earlobe, then passing the ring through the hole at the opening, and turning the gap downwards. Jade *huang* was arc-shaped, with a small hole drilled in one end for threading, and was used as a chest ornament or a neckpiece, same as the jade tubes and beads. Fish vertebrae were also made into such ornaments by polishing them, enlarging the round hole in the middle, and threading a string through them. Another type of ornaments was made of the horns of animals such as Reeves's muntjacs. The teeth of fierce beasts such as tigers, bears, and wild boars were also a good material. Since the hunting of these animals required great courage and wisdom, the person who was able to wear them was naturally regarded as a hero with courage and wisdom.

Another kind of pendants was the round carved ivory dagger, which was very rare. It was made in the shape of a bird with a long tail, resembling an eagle soaring in the sky overlooking the land. Ivory was so delicate and hard that it was not easy to work it in prehistoric times without metal tools. The tusks were first sliced into long strips of the right size, cut into shape roughly using tools such as stone axes, then ground to produce a semi-finished product, and finally carefully carved with a pattern. After these complex processes, an exquisite round carved ivory dagger was completed. It was a masterpiece of the Hemudu people's superb carving skills. The ivory bone dagger had a small hole on the ridge to string through, so that it could be worn as a decoration. But such an elaborate ornament was probably only worn by clan leaders or heroes as a symbol of status.

The Hemudu ancients' pursuit of beauty was not confined to the decoration of their bodies, but was extended to the decoration of various everyday objects, in which practicality and esthetics were achieved in perfect harmony. Decoration was found on almost all types of pottery, bone, and wood objects. Pottery was decorated with intricate patterns, for example, cord patterned, stamped and impressed with geometric designs, painted with animal images, and coated with slip. The cord pattern was initially left in a process to strengthen the pottery wall before the pottery was dry, during which the clay paddle wrapped with cords would leave traces of patting on the pottery surface. Later, the ancients found that the regular cord pattern was beautiful, so it was retained as a means of decoration. The cord pattern was only found on the belly and bottom of the pottery *fu*, while other vessels were scraped and polished to remove the cord pattern. In some cases, however, because of the sloppy scraping and polishing, faint traces of the cord pattern could still be seen on the surface. Geometric patterns were carved, stamped, or impressed with bone awls, bone tubes, plant branches, or shell edges. They include the string pattern, the shell pattern, the grain pattern, the ring pattern, the leaf pattern, and short diagonal lines. The ancients chose these plain patterns and combined them in different ways to create a rich and colorful decoration. In the 4th cultural layer of the Hemudu Site alone, for example, there were 104 distinct combinations of patterns. Most of these motifs were found on the shoulders and rims of *fu* vessels, the shoulders and bases of *yu* vessels, the necks of some jars, the rims of plates, the spindle whorls, and the *bo* with an inverted curved rim. The neck of some of the *fu* was occasionally comb patterned with a fine-toothed comb. The art of painted pottery was also a means of pottery decoration. A dense, even layer of gray "slip", namely a slurry of clay and water, was applied on the surface, with black and brown-black broad leaf patterns painted on top, resulting in a novel composition and brilliant colors.

With the passage of time, by about 6,000 years ago, pottery decoration was gradually simplified and reduced. Most of the pottery was plain without any decorative patterns. But some new decorative techniques appeared, such as the application of red or black pottery coating (黑色陶衣), openwork, and raised stripes. The pottery coating refers to applying a layer of slip on the exterior of the pottery. If this high iron content slip was fired in a strong oxidizing environment, the surface of the vessel would be bright red, known as red slip pottery; if it was fired in a reducing environment, its surface would be black, known as black slip pottery. The openwork is mainly found on the handle of the *dou*, with curved edge triangular and round holes. The raised stripe pattern is mostly found on the shoulders of the red slip pottery *fu*. Decorative methods popular in earlier periods, such as incising and stamping (刻划戳印), were still in use.

In addition to geometric patterns, jars, pots, and bowls were occasionally carved on the abdomen with extensive patterns of seedlings, grains, leaves, as well as pigs, fish, and other creatures, all of which were closely related to life. These patterns are regarded by many as the paintings of the Hemudu ancients. Most of the pottery ware were finely crafted and beautifully shaped, with simple but vivid images of animals and plants depicted with smooth lines, expressing the makers' meticulous observation of nature and praise for a good life. Among the extensive subjects, the number of plant motifs such as grains, leaf veins, flowers, and seeds reflecting the agricultural and gathering economy accounted for a much greater proportion of the total, than those of animal subjects reflecting the fishing and hunting economy. A typical example was the rectangular container carved on the front of a saddle-shaped pottery block, represented by a double line rectangle. In the container was a plant with five large leaves, one upright in the middle and two on each side, and beneath were roots illustrated with diagonal lines. The whole image was formed with simple, clear, bold, and powerful lines. On another brick-shaped pottery block was also carved a rectangular vessel containing a similar plant, with three thick leaves on the front and a leaf-bud on the side. It is thought that these two pieces of pottery indicate that the ancients had already been growing plants in pots, and that the five-leaved and three-leaved plants were the evergreens *Rohdea japonica*, expressing people's pray for a good crop. On the bottom of a pottery *bo*, four symmetrical leaves were depicted, with the petioles linked at the center and the four leaf tips almost quartering the circumference. On the outer wall of a pottery basin, a ripe rice plant was carved, with one ear of rice standing upright in the middle and the other ears drooping to the sides symmetrically, giving a vivid image of a good harvest. Among animal motifs, pigs and fish were the most common subjects. On a rectangular pottery *bo*, two similar pig patterns were carved on the two long sides, with a long pouting mouth, a swinging tail, curly hair on the body, and a vertical mane on the back, all fully expressed with powerful strokes. On the outer wall of a large, shiny black pottery basin, a group of fish among algae patterns were carved, seemingly swimming back and forth leisurely. Although not very realistic, the design was ingenious and interesting, showing a vivid scene. There was also a turtle-shaped pottery *he*. Its top looked like the shape of a turtle; its head was raised high with an open mouth, its curly tail carved with a fire pattern (火焰纹), its back decorated with symmetrical grain patterns, and the upper abdomen carved with pigs and deer, all with distinctive features. The entire pottery was a masterpiece with delicately incised designs made up of smooth lines, indicating the high artistic and ideological level of the Hemudu culture. In addition, on a pottery shard, two fish or maybe snakes were carved with smooth lines on the top and bottom, their heads facing each other and the bodies curving, forming a beautiful picture. These pieces, including the fish-and-algae basin (鱼藻纹 盆), the rice-ear basin, the square *bo* with the pig motif, the turtle-shaped pottery *he* (龟形陶盉), and the pottery block with a five-leaved plant, were among the best, reflecting the good wishes of the Hemudu ancients for a good agricultural harvest and prosperous husbandry.

Some small pottery sculptures of relatively simple shapes were likely to be pottery toys. They were often in imitation of everyday utensils like *fu*, jars, pots, plates, and *bo*, or animals, mostly half the size of a ping-pong ball or the size of an egg for some larger ones. Such small pottery pieces could not have had any practical value but for fun. Presumably, the children who followed the adults in the process of pottery making, plucked a bit from the clay, or used the leftover clay, to imitate the adults, and casually modeled them. Many such pieces were excavated, and we have to rely on our imagination to figure out their shapes, probably sheep, dogs, or birds, with the exception of a small pottery pig, which was vividly depicted with a drooping belly.

Some pottery pieces were more realistic, such as the pottery fish, whose two fins, covered with poked circles as scales, spread like wings, suggesting it was swimming. But there was also a larger piece of pottery sculpture, whose shape was rather odd. When a pile of crumbled pottery fragments unearthed was restored, an odd figure came into being, with four thick legs, a body densely carved with designs of circles, grain, arcs, grids, and woven patterns. Some view it as an "elephant". Another pottery sculpture with a similar shape was used as a *fu* support, and its side view looked like an elephant with a long trunk, but unfortunately, the "trunk" was severely damaged.

Relievo on the pottery was also a means of decoration frequently used by the Hemudu ancients, mostly describing small animals such as birds and insects. For example, on the rim of one pottery *bo*, the relief image of a small creeping salamander was carved. On the lid of another pottery vessel was a relief carving of two swallows fluttering their wings as if they were flying freely in the sky. Stamping was another means of decoration, mostly used to depict human faces. For instance, round impressions of different sizes and shapes were stamped on a remnant pottery button representing the human eyes, nose, and mouth, and the same pattern appeared on a trumpet-shaped *fu* stand. On a lovely pottery sculpture of a small animal, the inverted triangular face was stamped with circles representing the eyes, nostrils, and mouth. Though these images were relatively crude in appearance, they captured the essential characteristic of the object depicted and were vividly shaped, showing the Hemudu people's well-developed craft of pottery making.

The decorative motifs on bone tools were simpler than those on pottery but no less beautiful. In some cases, the handles of production tools and certain parts of household objects were decorated with simple geometric patterns consisting of an incised string pattern and diagonal lines. There were also a few intaglioed or drilled images of birds or other animals. Patterns of round impressions were the most common decoration on bone tools, some as the center of the design, some carved on both sides of the central pattern as a symmetrical decoration, some used to represent the animal eyes, and some smaller, denser ones forming a whole animal image.

Among the bone vessels, the most exquisite were the ivory carvings, especially the various round carvings. They represented the highest artistic level of the Hemudu culture.

Ivory, a precious material, has a fine and hard texture. It was really amazing that as early as about 7,000 years ago, the Hemudu ancients were able to produce exquisite ivory products through cutting, chopping, grinding and carving, using only rudimentary stone and bone tools.

The ivory carvings of the Hemudu culture were distinguished by their delicacy and beauty resulting from fine grinding and carving. A special type of them was made in the shape of a bird with spread wings, called bird-shaped or butterfly-shaped objects. They were not only finely polished, but also intricately incised with decorations on the front. On one such ware, five concentric circles representing the sun were carved on the front, with a circle of short radial lines around the periphery symbolizing sun rays. Another was very smoothly polished, finely carved with a similar sun image on the front and flame patterns around the periphery to symbolize the blazing flames of the sun, as well as two symmetrical birds with long beaks on each side, singing and looking to each other. Two round carved cap-shaped ivory objects were found, oval on the outside with a rectangular hole cut in the middle. They may have been used as a decorative accessory for some kind of handle with a tenon top, with the tenon fitting into the rectangular hole, and the small circular holes drilled in the side acting as the dowel hole. The outside of their brim was carved with a circle of woven patterns and small crawling silkworms.

In addition to round carved birds, incised birds were found on ivory as well, showing similarities with the former type. Another piece of ivory carving enjoyed the same fame as the butterfly-shaped ivory object of two birds facing the sun. It was a handle that had broken away from a bone dagger. Two similar double-headed birds were carved on it, each centered on a round impression. The two heads of both birds, with sharp pointed beaks, faced opposing directions instead of looking at each other as in the design on the previous artifact. The two double-headed birds were noted for the smooth and delicate incising and the balanced but lively composition of the design.

Wooden objects were often only polished yet rarely decorated. The main decorating methods were incising, carving, and lacquering. For instance, the tip for hand grip of a T-shaped wooden handle was vividly carved with a fish in great detail. The rest of the handle was also incised with parallel horizontal lines alternating with short diagonal lines. As for carving on wood components, for example, a board with a small tenon at each end was carved with two symmetrical double circles, and horizontal and diagonal lines on either side. Another board with flat tenons at both ends was carved with an elephant motif on the front. Its long trunk curled forward and looked like an "S", and its body was carved with circular motifs, leaf buds, and short diagonal lines as decoration. The upper and lower ends of this board were carved with string patterns with leaf buds in the middle. In addition, a wooden panel was excavated, on one side of which was carved a large animal with short, stout legs. But unfortunately, the head was missing, so it was difficult to identify the animal. These wood components, generally with tenons at both ends, were likely to have been used as decorative elements in the construction of houses.

The main carving techniques used in woodwork were open-work carving and round carving. The open-work carving was represented by the wood carved ritual object with double bird motif. The round carving was represented by the vivid small wooden fish.

The final process for making wood objects such as wooden bowls, cylinders, and bird-shaped vessels was the lacquering of the surface. The history of lacquerware production in China was quite long. According to ancient texts, such as the chapter "Shiguo" ("十过") in *Hanfeizi* (《韩非子》) and *Shuoyuan* (《说苑》), lacquer was used as early as in the legendary times of sages Shun (舜) and Yu (禹). At that time, red and black lacquer had been made by adding cinnabar and charcoal into the sap, and lacquerware was often a symbol of status instead of utensils for daily use by average people. Archeological findings at Hemudu show that the use of lacquerware in China came into use much earlier than what was recorded in those books, and that at least 7,000 years ago it was used by the Hemudu ancients.

In the Hemudu culture, lacquer was applied to the surface of wooden body, finely crafted and carefully polished. Some vessels were lacquered as a whole, but some were lacquered only partly. The lacquered bowl was generally small, of similar size to the small rice bowl nowadays. Its exterior was made into an oval shape with vertical ridges, a rounded space was cut out in the middle and a foot ring was attached at the bottom, and finally, a layer of red lacquer was applied to the surface. According to the Institute of Polymer Research of the Chinese Academy of Sciences, the scientific identification proved that this red paint was similar to that of the lacquer layer excavated from the Mawangdui Han Tomb Site (马王堆汉墓遗址 [1]), which led to the worldwide recognition of the lacquerware of the Hemudu culture. The wooden cylinder was a section cut from a thick wood 34 centimeters long and over 20 centimeters in diameter and hollowed in the middle; or perhaps it was cut in half and hollowed out and then glued together, like a bamboo tube. The inner wall was divided into several sections and round wood blocks were inserted in the middle. The two ends of the outer wall were lacquered and tied with rattan strips, or tied with rattan strips first and then lacquered. The delicate lacquered surface had a slight golden luster. These cylinders were notable for their unusual shape and elaborate processing. The bird-shaped (butterfly-shaped) artifact was flat and

---

[1]　The Mawangdui Han Tomb Site is located beside the Liuyang River, four kilometers east of Furong District, Changsha City, Hunan Province. It was the family tomb site of Li Cang (利仓), the chengxiang (丞相, prime minister) of the State of Changsha, in the early Western Han Dynasty. In the three tombs, Li Cang, his wife and his son were buried. The site was excavated in the 1970s. In total, over 3,000 relics, including one well-preserved female corpse, coffins, silk fabrics, silk books, silk paintings, lacquerware and herbal medicines, were unearthed from the tombs. The discovery of the Mawangdui Han Tomb Site provides important information for the study of the burial system, the development of handicrafts and technology and the history, culture and social life of the State of Changsha in the early Han Dynasty.

shaped either like a bird flying with its wings outstretched or like a standing bird, polished and lacquered on the outside. In some cases, the entire front of the bird-shaped artifact was lacquered, while in others, only the round impression or its peripheral circle on the two sides was painted with lacquer. These lacquerware from the Hemudu culture were the earliest ones ever found in China, dating from about 7,000 years ago, about 4,000 years earlier than the lacquerware from the Han tombs at the Mawangdui Site.

XII. Sun God's Hometown

In the early days of humankind, people were unable to make scientific explanations for the causes of changeable natural phenomena, and often attributed their successes and failures in life to natural forces. Gain was seen as a gift from nature, loss a punishment. To bring spiritual comfort, natural phenomena were super-naturalized and deified, and thus the earliest religious concepts emerged. The objects of worship included celestial bodies such as the sun, the moon, and stars, natural forces like wind, rain, thunder, and lightning, and natural objects such as mountains, rivers, stones, trees, birds, beasts, fish, and insects. All these were closely related to the ancients' production and life, and were believed to have special mysterious powers. Their worship was expressed through artwork such as bone carvings, tooth carvings, wood carvings, and pottery sculptures, by which their beliefs, emotions, custom, and prayers were communicated.

The Hemudu people also worshiped the things in nature. Many of their pottery, bone, and wood artifacts were decorated with animal, plant, and sun motifs, or even carved into animal figures. Among the decorations, the images of birds and the sun appeared most frequently. And the artifacts with these images were the most exquisite, reflecting the people's worship of birds and the sun.

In the Hemudu culture, artifacts with images of birds, the sun, and the combination of them were excavated in large numbers, such as the vessel lid with a modeled design of double swallows (双飞燕), the wood carved bird-shaped artifacts, the wood carved ritual object with double bird motif, the ivory carved dagger handle with conjoined bird motif, the ivory carved dagger with bird motif, the ivory carved bird-shaped artifact with sun motif, and the ivory carved bird-shaped artifact with sun motif. These artifacts far exceeded those with animal motifs such as pigs, dogs, sheep, and fish in terms of number, the quality of the materials, and the exquisiteness of the carving, which was a phenomenon extremely rare in other prehistoric sites. A few of these pieces already were bold creations based on imagination beyond realistic portrayal, reflecting the Hemudu people's mysterious spiritual world.

On the lid of a vessel, the modeled design of "double swallows" seemed to be flying freely in the air, with their heads held high and wings raised. The wood carved bird-shaped artifacts, carved out of a whole piece of wood, were divided into two types: one with symmetrical wings and the other with asymmetrical wings. The former type was either painted with black lacquer all over, though most of which had fallen off, or painted only at the round impressions near the root of the bird's wings or the circles around. The other type was characterized by its standing-bird form (立鸟形状), one wing carved into an eagle's head, with a thick, blunt hooked beak and a round impression on the front as the eye, and the other wing made into a polygonal or curled bird tail. The wood carved ritual object with double bird motif was also carved out of a single wood panel. The two birds, each with a long thick hooked beak and an eye depicted with a round impression, were carved on the two wings of the artifact respectively, with their backs toward each other. Their bodies were decorated with two ring patterns, and their thick tails were spread and connected to each other. The lower part of the panel was carved into two claws. The external outline of this artifact was the same as that of the symmetrical, wood carved bird-shaped (butterfly-shaped) artifacts. It is likely, therefore, that the two wings of those symmetrical bird-shaped artifacts each represent a bird; with the spread wings and the round impression near the root of the wing being the eye, the whole artifact showed a large bird composed of two conjoined birds (连体双鸟) with their heads turned back to each other.

The handle of the bone dagger with a motif of conjoined birds carved on the front was also worth our attention. The two heads on the same body were tilted back. Their beaks resembled that of an eagle. Their large eyes were represented by shallow round impressions. The back, shaped into a mountain peak, looked like a burning flame. Similar round impressions were also carved in the center of the body. Each side of the bird motif was decorated with alternating string patterns and with diagonal lines. Several similar ivory carved daggers with bird motif were found, with a total of 5 from the Hemudu Site, 1 from the Zishan Site, and a number of fragments from the Tianluoshan Site. Their forms were almost identical. The front of the handle was the head, the middle of the handle was the broad rectangular body, whose front was carved with a motif consisting of string patterns and diagonal lines, and the long blade, accounting for two thirds of the length, was the exaggerated tail. Viewed from the side, it looks like a bird with an eagle's beak, large eyes, a short belly, and a long tail, all finely carved. On the belly was a horizontal ridge with a round hole drilled through and traces of threading. On one such dagger, the original hole was broken, and a new hole was made in the same position. These bone daggers were rare pieces of art, carefully carved and polished, cleverly designed with exaggerated shapes, clear outlines, and a vivid three-dimensional effect. The bird-shaped ivory vessels had an inverted convex shape with rounded corners. Two types of vessels were excavated, either decorated with the sun-pattern only or decorated with the motif of double birds in the shining sun. The former type was polished on the front, with a small round impression drilled in the upper middle and five concentric circles carved around it symbolizing the sun, as well as short lines surrounding the outermost circle as its rays. The upper part of the two wings were carved with a crescent-shaped hole respectively, on the outer side of which was carved a small round impression, and the periphery of the lower part was carved with four string patterns with short lines in between, the inner side of which was carved with an arc made up of five lines. The latter type also had a polished front and was carved with two birds and the sun, which was depicted by a small round impression surrounded by five concentric circles. Above the sun was a "flame" pattern, symbolizing the flames of the blazing sun. Two symmetrical birds with long hooked beaks were looking back at each other. The outlines of the birds were clear and smooth as a result of the marvelous carving skills. The small round impressions at the center of the bird''s head were the eyes, two small circular holes were drilled at different intervals on each side of the head, one small circular hole was drilled in the lower part on each side, and between the holes were arc patterns made up of slanted lines with string patterns in between. There are many similar ivory bird-shaped artifacts, 17 found at the Hemudu Site alone, and many more at the Tianluoshan Site. Although all made of precious ivory, which was hard and delicate in texture and difficult to carve, they were all very finely polished, with fine and intricate ornamentation on the front, reflecting the high artistic creativity and rich imagination of the Hemudu ancients.

There was also an eagle-shaped pottery *dou*. The head and the tail were carved at the two opposing tips of the rim, and the symmetrical wings on the sides seemed as if the eagle was fluttering its wings. The details were carefully dealt with — a hooked beak, two nostrils expressed by small holes drilled through the beak, and widely open eyes. The round carved ivory eagle head was especially vivid, with a broad nose, a hooked beak, and rounded eyes, showing an intimidating force.

A total of more than 60 pieces of artifacts with designs of birds, the sun, and the combination of them were excavated from the Hemudu culture, among which bird-shaped wooden artifacts, over 30 pieces, accounted for the most, followed by over 20 pieces of bird-shaped ivory artifacts, seven or eight pieces of round carved ivory daggers, and two pieces of other types. The discovery of so many bird-related cultural relics shows that the Hemudu ancients had special feelings and affections for birds, and strongly proves their reverence of birds and worship of bird totems. The term "totem" was originally a native language of the North American Indians, meaning "his kin", worshiped as the ancestor of the clan and regarded as its symbol and protector.

The ancients closely associated the birds with the sun (双鸟朝阳), as is reflected in the bird-shaped ivory artifact with two birds facing the sun and the bone dagger handles with conjoined birds. The sun in the former design was depicted as a ball of light and heat, as the short lines around the outer circle were removed and replaced with a flame pattern. What was even more peculiar was the birds on either side of the sun, which were not afraid of heat or fire and even became one with the sun. They might be divine birds endowed with extraordinary powers, a part of the sun, or the flight instruments that carried the sun on their backs. Similarly, the "conjoined birds" on the bone dagger handle, though flying with their backs turned to each other, had the sun in the middle, which was shining in all directions as if uniting all into one.

A legend has been recorded in the ancient Chinese books — *Shanhaijing* (《 山海经 》 , *The Classics of Mountains and Rivers*) and in the chapter "Tianwenpian" (" 天文篇 ", "The Chapter on Astronomy") of *Huainanzi* — saying that "in the tree of the Tang Valley (汤谷), two suns carried on the backs of crows rest by turns". The carvings on the above-mentioned cultural relics were consistent with this ancient Chinese legend. They perhaps depicted the extraordinary birds in this legend — the sun-carrying three-legged crows. How did the Hemudu ancients come up with this idea? When they saw the morning sun rise in the east and the evening sun set in the west over and over again, they believed that the sun was able to cross the sky with the help of other means of transport, and that the only things that soared in the sky together with the sun, the moon and stars were birds. Thus, they associated the two with each other. In their legend, this pair of birds that could fly with the sun on their back were certainly sacred birds.

These images of birds and sun mentioned above were creatively conceived in the Hemudu people's rich imagination, and reflected their sun worship.

Sun worship was a primitive religious practice widespread during the Neolithic Period around the world. Many ancient peoples around the world had their own sun gods, such as the ancient Egyptians, who worshiped the sun god Aten, the ancient Greeks, who created the sun god Apollo (阿波罗), the ancient Indians, who believed in the sun goddess Surya [also known as Aditya (阿狄多)], and the Babylonians, who worshiped the sun god Shamash (沙马士). The different environments around the world produced different primitive cultures, but there were many common elements in the creation of sun gods. For instance, the crown of light arrows worn on the sun god in the Mayan culture of Central and South America is similar to the "sun crown" on the bone dagger handle with conjoined birds; Apollo's wings and the two birds protecting the sun on the bird-shaped ivory artifact also share something in common. These similarities resulted from different peoples' exploration of nature and the low level of productivity in ancient times. The bird-shaped artifacts, like legends of Aditya or Apollo, are a precious treasure of mankind.

Apart from the mystery of the rising and falling every day and the light and warmth brought by the sun, the Hemudu people's sun worship was most closely related to their primitive agriculture. As a Chinese saying goes, "The growth of everything depends on the sun." In their long-term agricultural production, they gradually realized the important role of the sun in agriculture. So they worshiped and sacrificed to the sun god, praying for a good agricultural harvest. It is assumed that the elaborate bird-shaped ivory artifact with two birds facing the sun were crafted for ritual purposes, worshiped as the symbol of the sun god in the sacrifice.

The burial custom also reflected the primitive religious concept of the Hemudu ancients. In the Neolithic Period, people of a clan lived in the same place and were mostly buried in clan graves after death. At first, there was no significant difference in the quantity and quality of burial goods, but later, a disparity would grow between the rich and the poor. The burial system and burial custom can more or less reflect the social system, social relations, social economy, and religious ideology of the time, and are often regarded as a microcosm of the social life then. The burials of the Hemudu culture were divided into two categories: those scattered around houses and those buried in clan graves.

No clan cemetery was found in the early Hemudu culture, and only two pottery *fu* and jars were found with the mixed remains of infants and fish bones inside. Later on, burials scattered around houses were found, but no burial pits or burial tools were found, and most of them had no burial objects. The bones were well preserved, the majority belonging to infants and people under age, but the skull or limbs were commonly incomplete. In the late period of the Hemudu culture, burials were also found scattered around houses, without burial tools or burial goods. In those rectangular shaft tombs, human bones were poorly preserved, many with incomplete skulls or limbs, and were generally laid on the back with straight limbs. The burial system was a reflection of the concept of the immortality of the soul. Generally, those who died normally enjoyed regular burial treatment, such as being buried in a clan grave, while those who died abnormally did not, and some of them did not even have the opportunity to enter the graves of normal death. In the case of burials scattered around the houses, according to the incomplete skulls or limbs inside, perhaps they were tombs of people who died before adulthood or from other accidental causes.

Only one clan cemetery was found at the Tashan Site, and most of the 50 tombs were rectangular shaft tombs, divided into two types: primary burials and secondary burials. The skeletons of the secondary burials were generally arranged in their original state (in a straight-limbed supine position), with scattered piles of funerary objects, mainly pottery and a small number of decorative jade pieces. Among them, the 40 burials beneath the 9th cultural layer were divided into three categories according to the burial objects, category A with *dou*, category B with *fu*, and category C with neither. There were significant differences between the location and the direction of category A and category B graves. At the Xiangjiashan Site, a concentration of "urn burials" were found around a round earth platform of red burned clay, with charcoal and burned white bone fragments around the platform and the urn burials.

A very interesting phenomenon in the burials of the Hemudu culture that deserves our attention is that whether in scattered burials around houses or in burials of a communal cemetery, most of the human skulls faced east. Twenty-seven scattered burials were found at the Hemudu Site, among which 22 have skulls identifiable tomb direction. Eighteen of the skulls faced east, east-south, or east-north. Among the over 50 burials found at the Tashan cemetery, 40 burials had recognizable skulls, all of which faced east, east-south, or east-north. The east is where the sun rises, so the skulls in the burials of the Hemudu culture might have been arranged to face the direction where the sun rises. But why were some of the skulls in the tombs of the Hemudu culture facing east-south or east-north? It was because the sun does not always rise due east throughout the year, but sometimes to the south and sometimes to the north, depending on the season. Thus, the fact that the Hemudu ancients oriented the skulls in burials roughly towards the east was also a form of sun worship. If we further combine this with the ancient concept of the immortality of the soul and the concept of seeing death as life, we could realize that the skulls of the deceased were oriented towards the east in the hope that they would receive the warmth and light of the sun even after death. They held the view that one's life meant the rising and setting of the sun, and the sun would rise in the next morning as usual.

XIII. The Origins and Evolution of the Hemudu Culture

The Hemudu culture was famous for its well-developed rice farming with *si*-tillage, superb wooden stilt houses, and complex tenon-and-mortise work, as well as unique charcoal-tempered black pottery. One may wonder, then, where did the Hemudu ancients come from, and where did they go after having created such a splendid culture? Regarding the first question, there are two possibilities: it either originated locally, or migrated from other places. Other statements about the origin were summarized as either "the mountains theory" and "the sea theory", which were in fact not substantially different from the two earlier ones. The former speculates that the Hemudu culture started in the foothills of mountains on the southern edge of the Ningbo-Shaoxing Plain; the latter believes that the Hemudu culture originated in places 5–6 meters below current sea level on the continental shelf near the sea, or places now buried a few meters below the Ningbo-Shaoxing Plain, before its people migrating to the current sites of the Hemudu culture. For a long time, neither of the two theories could convince each other due to the lack of reliable scientific evidence.

Both theories analyzed the origins of this culture from the perspective of natural environment evolution in the Ningbo-Shaoxing area since the last ice age. As already mentioned, the last marine transgressions began about 12,000 years ago, when the sea rose slowly, gradually flooded the low-lying coastal plains, penetrated deeper into the interior land, and reached its highest more than 8,000 years ago. As a result, the present-day Ningbo Plain became a shallow sea. It was not until about 7,400 years ago that the sea level began to fall, and the Yuyao-Cicheng Plain, where the Yuyao River Valley was located, became a land. Though there were several subsequent drops in sea level, the effect on surrounding areas was not significant. Therefore, the "mountain theory" holds that humans could not have lived in the flooded areas now called Ningbo Plain, and that the mountainous areas and foothills in the south of the Ningbo-Shaoxing Plain, especially the mountain basins of various sizes south of Shaoxing, could have been more suitable habitats.

In the 21st century, exciting archeological discoveries in the mountains and foothills of the southern Ningbo-Shaoxing Plain have been made one after another. The discovery and excavation of the Shangshan Site in Pujiang County, Zhejiang Province, and the Xiaohuangshan Site in Shengzhou County, Zhejiang Province pushed the upper limit of the Neolithic Period in Zhejiang to more than 10,000 years ago, and encouraged the search for the origins of the Hemudu culture. The development of the Xiaohuangshan Site is divided into three phases, and the remains of its latest phase, such as its cord-patterned ring-footed *fu* and flat-footed jar with two ears (双耳平底罐), shared some similarities with some pottery vessels from the Hemudu culture. So it can be assumed that the third phase of the culture at the Xiaohuangshan Site could be an important source for the Hemudu culture. But there is still a long way to go before evidence for the direct source from which the Hemudu culture developed is found.

The "sea theory" can also be justified by the geographical evolution. When the marine transgression first began, the sea level was still at a depth of more than 100 meters under the present-day seawater, and the coastline at that time was approximately at the edge of the continental shelf east of the Zhoushan Islands. Therefore, the sea around the islands was still a land. In recent years, fishermen have often recovered ancient animal bones from the shallow waters around the Zhoushan Islands. Especially in 2002, over 120 fossils of mammals were found at a depth of about 96 meters in the waters near Jintang Town (金塘镇), among which 4 of the antlers were found to have been artificially hacked and cut. It indicated that at least 10,000–30,000 years ago, this area, now submerged in the sea, was still land, suitable not only for four-legged mammals, but also for primitive humans. Marine transgressions are different from tsunamis. Tsunamis instantly send up huge waves tens of meters high, quickly engulfing the coastal area and causing havoc for the people there. Marine transgressions, on the other hand, are relatively slow. The sea with a depth of 100 meters around the Zhoushan Islands was the result of a slow rise over thousands of years. And although the rise of sea level was sometimes quick and sometimes slow, on average it was within a few centimeters per year. Therefore, there was plenty of time for humans to move to higher ground before the sea flooded their villages, the so-called "sea in and man out". Many of the original villages were lost to the sea, and those on the Ningbo-Shaoxing Plain were buried several meters or even tens of meters below the surface of the sea, so that they were not easily found by later generations. When the sea receded, people returned to the mountainous plains of the Ningbo-Shaoxing Plain with their families, and these people were believed to be the Hemudu ancients.

For the lack of further archeological evidence, it is difficult to determine which theory is right under the present circumstances. Another problem that bothers us as much as the origin of the Hemudu culture is that about 5,300 years ago, the Hemudu culture in the Ningbo area suddenly disappeared and the Liangzhu culture took its place soon. One might ask: where did their descendants go? Some contend that the Hemudu ancients were relocated en masse due to floods or other disasters, and later the people of the Liangzhu culture around Taihu Lake moved en masse into the Ningbo area. In fact, this is a misinterpretation of culture in the archeological sense. An analogy will clarify what this means. A student who used a pencil for writing in primary school may use a fountain pen in middle school. The difference between pencils and fountain pens is obvious, but their user might be the same person. The relationship between the Hemudu culture and the Liangzhu culture is similar to that of pencil and pen; that is, the descendants of the Hemudu culture still lived in the area, but their household utensils, production tools, and so on changed dramatically. However, some of the traditional elements and influences of the Hemudu culture were retained in the descendants' life, such as the cord pattern pottery *fu*, which were still used as cooking utensils and buried in tombs as funerary objects. It seems that some traditional concepts, customs, and other ideological factors of the Hemudu culture were deeply rooted in the mind of their descendants.

As early as around 6,000 years ago, the prehistoric culture of the northern shore of Hangzhou Bay started to influence primitive humans in the Ningbo area. This influence became more and more evident later on. Finally, the primitive people in Ningbo integrated into the Liangzhu culture around 5,300 years ago. Of course, the process of influence was not limited to specific artifacts such as everyday utensils and production tools. Abstract things like religion and custom were also important factors leading to the integration, and another direct contributor might be population migration, which was motivated by both environmental and social reasons.

Around 6,000 years ago or earlier, part of the Hemudu descendants remained in the local area, and some migrated outwards, both by land and by sea. The land route led south through Xianju, Yueqing to Taishun, and the coastal route led south through Taizhou to Wenzhou. The first stop by sea was Zhoushan Islands; the second stop was Zhoushan Islands, Qushan Island (衢山岛) of Zhoushan Islands, Gaotang Island (高塘岛) in Xiangshan County, and Beilong Island (北龙岛) in Rui'an County; the third stop by sea was Keqiutou on Pingtan Island in Fujian Province.

In 1982, a ring-footed cord pattern sand-tempered pottery *fu* was excavated from the waters near Dazhushan Island (大竹山岛) of the Miaodao Islands of Shandong Province. The vessel was similar to the pottery *fu* of the fourth period Hemudu culture. And Dazhushan Island could be regarded as the northernmost point of the distribution of the Hemudu culture relics.

The distribution area of the Hemudu culture was geographically a self-contained and relatively independent area. To the south were the Siming Mountains, the Tiantai Mountains, and the smaller hills of Zhejiang and Fujian, obstacles in its exchange with the prehistoric cultures of Fujian Province and Guangdong Province; to the east was the endless sea; to the west was the surging Cao'e River; to the north was the turbulent Hangzhou Bay. However, these natural obstacles did not prevent the Hemudu ancients from interacting with the outside world. With the use of primitive water vehicles such as canoes and bamboo (wooden) rafts, the Hemudu ancients carried out extensive exchanges with primitive cultures in their neighborhood, and passed many advanced production and living styles onto the succeeding cultures, thus contributing greatly to the formation of ancient Chinese civilization.

The area around Taihu Lake on the northern shore of Hangzhou Bay was home to the Majiabang culture and the Songze culture, which were roughly contemporaneous with the Hemudu culture. The Majiabang culture, named after the site of Majiabang in Jiaxing City excavated in 1959, existed for over 1,500 years. The Hemudu culture and the Majiabang culture were separated only by Hangzhou Bay, and their natural environmental conditions were similar in many ways. So, relying on primitive water vehicles such as canoes and bamboo (wooden) rafts, they interacted with and learned from each other during their development.

In the earliest stages of the Hemudu culture and the Majiabang culture, the influence of the former on the latter was dominant. But around 6,000 years ago, this situation was fundamentally reversed. This was due to the fact that the western and northern areas of the Majiabang culture in the Taihu Basin were flat and therefore it was relatively easy for the local people to communicate with the neighboring primitive cultures. The advanced productivity factors of the neighboring cultures in its west and north were well accepted, and as a result, the productivity of the Majiabang culture was improved. At this time, the status of the Hemudu culture changed from the initial transmitter of advanced civilization to the recipient. This one-way cultural diffusion became increasingly obvious and frequent over time, so that unless with careful investigation, the cultural landscape of the 3rd and 4th phases of the Hemudu culture would look very similar to that of the late Majiabang culture and the Songze culture, which is the reason why the

Hemudu Site was once estimated to belong to the Majiabang culture or the Songze culture right after its first excavation.

West of the Cao'e River is the area where the Shangshan culture and the Kuahuqiao culture were distributed. The Shangshan culture in Pujiang County had a history of more than 10,000 years, and the Kuahuqiao culture in Xiaoshan District, Hangzhou City had a history of about 8,000 years. Both of them were dated back earlier than the Hemudu culture. The prehistoric cultures of this area were complex, and at present no contemporaneous sites of the early stages of the Hemudu culture have been found. But 6,000 years ago in this area, the relationship between the Hemudu culture and Majiabang culture was surprisingly harmonious, while the early Shangshan culture and Kuahuqiao culture were not inherited by later generations. The reasons for this interesting phenomenon deserve further study.

In short, during its development, the Hemudu culture was in constant contact with the neighboring cultures, and many advanced factors of productivity were quickly spread in the cultural communication. The bones of whales, sharks, tunas, sea turtles, and other sea creatures found in the Hemudu culture fully indicated that the Hemudu ancients were already engaged in marine fishing activities with the help of primitive water vehicles, and were technically prepared for the movement to the Zhoushan Islands; at the same time, it also reflected that the prehistoric inhabitants of the southeastern coast already had a certain ability to sail, which undoubtedly created the conditions for spreading the fruits of the Hemudu culture to Southeast Asia, including stilt houses, lacquer paintings, stepped stone adzes, and double-hole stone knives.

Stilt houses with a lifted living space on an elevated base were the characteristic of the Hemudu culture. With people living above and livestock under the floor, these buildings could protect the residents against snakes, insects, and animals, and shield people from dampness and miasma. The unique form of such buildings was adapted to the humid and rainy climate of the south. In the sites of Late Neolithic Period, like the Qianshanyang Site (钱

山漾遗址) in Huzhou City, Zhejiang Province, the Longnan Site (龙南遗址) in Wuxian County, Jiangsu Province, and the Qingdun Site (青墩遗址) in Haian County, Jiangsu Province, there were also remains of stilt houses. A vessel excavated from the Xiantanmiao Site, Huzhou City, Zhejiang Province, has a line drawing of a stilt house carved on the inside of its lid. During the Xia, Shang, and Zhou Dynasties, stilt houses appeared in southern areas such as Maogang (茅冈) in Gaoyao District, Guangdong Province, Chengdu City, Sichuan Province, Maojiazui (毛家嘴) in Qichun County, Hubei Province, and Haimen (海门) in Jianchuan County, Yunnan Province. During the Qin and Han Dynasties, with the widespread distribution of metal tools and further improvement of carpentry techniques, stilt houses were developed to an unprecedented extent; remains of stilt houses of this period have been found in Jiangsu Province and Fujian Province, and pottery models of stilt houses and barns were also found as funerary objects in tombs of the Han Dynasty in provinces like Guangdong, Guangxi, Hunan, and Jiangsu. Moreover, models or images of stilt houses were found on bronze shell containers excavated at the Shizhaishan Site in Jinning District, Yunnan Province, and on the bronze *chun* (青铜錞) and drums excavated in Sichuan Province, further proving the widespread and long-lasting influence of stilt houses of the Hemudu culture. In modern times, stilt houses are still prevalent in the southwestern region of China, like the Guangxi Zhuang Autonomous Region. From the Yayoi-era stilt barns and watch towers found at the Yoshinogari Site (吉野里遗址) in Japan, it can be concluded that stilt houses already spread to Japan, the Philippines, and Taiwan of China at least 2,000 years ago.

China has a long history of using lacquerware. The lacquered wooden cylinders and lacquered wooden bowls found in the Hemudu culture were among the earliest lacquerware to date not only nationwide but also worldwide, thus pushing the upper limit of the use of lacquer in China back to the Neolithic Period, 7,000 years ago. Two trumpet-shaped lacquered wooden artifacts were later unearthed at the Weidun Site (圩墩遗址) in

Changzhou City. The black paint on their suface is slightly lustrous and looks the same as today's lacquer. In the middle layer of the Songze culture in Shanghai, lacquer-painted jars, pots, *dou*, cups, and other pottery were found in red-brown and yellowish colors, and in the Xiantanmiao Site in Haiyan County, lacquer-painted pottery pots and *dou* from the Songze culture were found. During the stage of the Liangzhu culture, in addition to the exquisite jade-inlaid lacquerware unearthed from the cemeteries of the Fanshan, Yaoshan (瑶山), and the Huiguanshan Site (汇观山遗址), lacquer-painted pottery and lacquer pieces were also frequently found in the areas of Maqiao Town (马桥镇) in Shanghai, Tuanjie Village (团结村) in Wujiang District, Jiangsu Province, and the Shuitianfan Site (水田畈遗址) in Gongshu District and Liangzhu Site in Yuhang District, both in Hangzhou, Zhejiang Province. The earliest jade-inlaid lacquer vessel known in China, a vermilion lacquer standing cup with inlaid jade from the Yaoshan Site, was unearthed with a decayed wood body, but the original lacquer coating was still evenly applied on the inner and outer walls, and remained intact and lustrous. A band of jade grains was inlaid on the outer wall at the junction of the body and ring foot of the cup and the place near the bottom of the ring foot. Among the prehistoric cultures outside the lower reaches of the Yangtze River, lacquerware were found in large numbers only at the Taosi Site (陶寺遗址) of the Longshan culture (龙南文化 , about 4,000 years ago) in Xiangfen County, Shanxi Province, where lacquer was used as a glue to fix the inlay on the wooden objects, head ornaments, and arm ornaments. The wooden body were perhaps painted with a layer of red lacquer on the plain surface, before patterns in cyan, green, yellow, blue, and white were painted on the red background. Many pieces of lacquered pottery ware were found, generally with red, white, or yellow band patterns, swirling patterns, and variant animal patterns painted on black coating. Given the lasting time of the Longshan culture, the Taosi Site cannot have been the birthplace of the lacquerware on the central plains. The use of lacquer in the lower reaches of the Yangtze River had a longer history and a more continuous development, indicating that the lower reaches of the Yangtze River must have been the origin of lacquerware in China, and the Hemudu ancients were more likely to be the discoverers and users of lacquer.

Stepped stone adzes were widely distributed in the vast areas on the western coast of the Pacific Ocean. Their shapes and the cultural context where they were used varied, and their functions were different, accordingly. Most of them had a narrow body, used as the tools for carpentry work, most often to dig canoes out of big wood trunks, occasionally as agricultural tools. It is now accepted that the arc-backed stepped stone adzes found in the Hemudu culture were the prototype of other stepped stone adzes. During the second and third periods of the Hemudu culture, the same arc-backed stepped stone adzes were also seen in some sites of the Majiabang culture in the Taihu Basin frequently. During the periods of the Songze culture and the Liangzhu culture, the stepped stone adze achieved unprecedented development in the lower reaches of the Yangtze River area, spread around and overseas gradually, and had a great impact on the cultures of the western Pacific coast, the southeastern islands, and the islands of the South Pacific during the Late Neolithic Period, and even the Bronze Age. In Jiangsu Province and Zhejiang Province, stepped stone adzes, as typical production tools of the Yue culture and the Baiyue culture (百越文化), were still found in the Shang Dynasty. It became gradually replaced during the Western Zhou Dynasty.

A number of broken rectangular double-hole stone knives were found in the Hemudu culture. In the Qianshanyang Site of the Liangzhu culture, they evolved into half-moon shaped double-hole stone knives, often with a curved back and a flat blade, or a flat and straight back and a curved blade, and were named after their half-moon shape. These stone knives were introduced northwards into Shandong Province of China, across the sea to the Korean Peninsula and even to Japan.

The development and spread of the stilt house, lacquerware, stepped stone adze, and double-hole stone knife not only influenced the primitive cultures around the Hemudu culture, but also had a profound impact on the primitive cultures of Southeast Asian countries and Japan later on. The spread of stepped stone adzes was the most typical of these influences. Along with their spread was the method of canoe making and the technique of sailing on rivers, lakes, and the sea, which could greatly enlarge primitive people's communication scope, for in the primitive times, limited by low level of productivity, people could communicate by water more easily, quickly, and widely than by land.

XIV. The Integration into the Liangzhu Culture

Around 5,300 years ago, the area around the Taihu Lake on the northern shore of Hangzhou Bay was developed to the stage of the Liangzhu culture. An ancient city of 2.9 million square meters was constructed, with tall buildings based on platforms, man-made altars, and high-profile tombs built for important people. Exquisite jade ritual objects such as the *cong*, *bi* (disks), and *yue* (battle-ax) were produced in great numbers. There, the first signs of "civilization" emerged. Meanwhile, the cultural landscape of Ningbo at this time also underwent a radical change, gradually fused with the Liangzhu culture in the long-term collision and exchange, and finally became a local type of it, called the Mingshanhou type or the southern type of the Liangzhu culture. In the beginning, people's activity scope in Ningbo was mainly restricted to the Yuyao-Cicheng Plain in the Yuyao River Region, the habitat of the Hemudu ancients. With the development of productivity, population growth, and changes in the natural environment, the people of Liangzhu culture in Ningbo began to settle in areas previously unsuitable for living, and their activity scope expanded greatly, resulting in significant changes in all aspects of production and life compared to the Hemudu culture.

The villages, located on slopes at a higher altitude, were smaller in size than those in the past, with only a few thousand square meters, the largest being less than twenty thousand square meters, but were more densely distributed in that they were located in close proximity to each other. They were generally abandoned when more suitable places were found, often after only a few decades, or after a hundred years at most. Usually, ground houses were built, with a trench-like foundation dug beforehand, filled with stones and clay; then earth walls were erected and finally covered with rafters and roofs. Such practice is still common in rural areas of modern Ningbo.

Another type of house was related to the stilt house. Pits were dug first, stone blocks were paved at the bottom in some cases, columns of varying sizes were buried in at different depths, the column pits were then filled with red burned clay, and finally, houses were built on the columns. At this time, around the Taihu Lake, there were semi-cave houses, but it is not known whether this was also the case in Ningbo.

During this period, earth platforms in the shape of an inverted funnel were built in Ningbo. One such platform was excavated, with a side length of 42.5 meters and a remaining height of 1.8 meters, surrounded by a deep ditch. The construction of this platform was preceded by a ritual of burning sacrificial offerings on a pile of firewood, leaving a large area of ashes at its base, which suggested the grandness and solemnity of the ritual. The platform was built with alternate layers of brownish-yellow sand and yellowish-brown clay, which made it very hard and solid. The rammer was made of 4 square logs tied together, each about 9 square centimeters in cross-section, and its square shape was clearly visible on the ground when the site was excavated. Unfortunately, the main part of the platform was destroyed, with only a small part in the north left. The 7 stone *yue* from inside the platform were collected, similar in shape and size, all very finely ground and carefully polished, with no openings or traces of use on the edges. So these stone *yue* were not likely to be practical tools, but were presumably burial objects in the platform. There were many such artificially built earthen platforms in the Liangzhu culture sites around the Taihu Lake, such as in the Fanshan Site (反山遗址) in Yuhang District, the Fuquanshan Site (福泉山遗址) in Shanghai, as well as the Zhanglingshan Site (张陵山遗址) and the Caoxieshan Site (草鞋山遗址) in Jiangsu Province. The earthen platforms were generally used to hold various rituals and bury the nobles. Therefore, this platform unearthed in Ningbo might also have been an altar and at the same time a burial place for the clergy who conducted the rituals. The Liangzhu culture in the Taihu Lake Basin had three burial forms, namely, being buried on a high earthen platform, in a clan cemetery, or sporadically around houses. It might also have been the same in Ningbo. However, limited by the current archeological discovery, only a very small number of small tombs buried sporadically around houses were found in Ningbo. These small, scattered tombs generally had shallow rectangular pits, in some cases even without pits. Only a few pottery objects were buried in them and the human skeletons were poorly preserved. The owners of these tombs were likely to be the toiling masses at the bottom of the social ladder.

Rice farming must have been an important economic activity for the Ningbo ancients. Though no physical rice was found, marks of rice were frequently found on the walls of the pottery, as evidence of the widespread rice cultivation. But the situation of other crops was less clear. The people of Liangzhu around the Taihu Lake had already started to grow mulberries, raise silkworms and reel silk, and plant sesame, peanuts, gourds, and melons, which were also very likely to be the varieties of crops in Ningbo then.

The development of agriculture at this time was marked by the emergence of new tools such as the stone plow, the stone plowshare, and the stone hoe. Stone plows were made in the form of isosceles triangles, or combined by three pieces, and increasingly larger stone plows were made later. Bone *si* and wooden *si* had to be used intermittently for soil turning, while stone plows, though similar in use, could turn the soil continuously, which greatly improved the efficiency of land tilling and was a sign of progress in rice farming. As for the stone plowshare, they were not field managing tools, as previously believed. The management of rice fields could only be carried out after the rice was already sown or planted in rows at regular intervals. As indicated by the name, the crown of the plough was the part to be subjected to a great deal of resistance. The stone plowshare was suitable for breaking up large blocks of soil turned up by stone plows, leveling fields, and weeding rice fields before the sowing. Although stone plowshares were not comparable to iron ones of later times, they were certainly more wear-resistant than those made of wood or bone. The stone hoe, also known as the "soil breaker" (破土器), had a single-edged blade and was roughly triangular in shape, with a badly worn, round front and a short, diagonal handle at the rear end. It first appeared in the Liangzhu culture and continued to be in use until the Zhou Dynasty, when the bronze hoe came into being, but possibly the latter was only a dry land farming tool. According to the traces of use on the blade, the stone hoe was a tool used in an oblique up-and-down motion for weeding instead of ditching and soil turning. Stone knives were made in a variety of sizes and shapes for different uses, including double-hole half-moon knives, long knives, double-shouldered knives, and boot-shaped knives. The long knives and double-hole half-moon knives were scythes, used to harvest rice ears, while the double-shouldered and boot-shaped knives were larger and heavier, probably kitchen knives, used to cut animal meat, various vegetables and fruits. Also related to agriculture is the pestle and mortar, which was used to hull the rice. Many large pottery mortars were found in sites of the Liangzhu culture, and the matching pestles were presumably made of wood like those of the Hemudu culture. The widespread use of pestles and mortars greatly improved the efficiency, and was a strong indication that rice farming had been well developed by that time.

No other domesticated animals than pigs, sheep, dogs, and cattle could have been raised by the Liangzhu people in Ningbo, according to archeological findings. Fishing, hunting, and gathering were still important sources of food at the time. But given that many villages were far from the mountains and close to rivers and lakes, fishing and collecting fruits from aquatic plants were obviously more important than hunting and wild fruits gathering in the mountain. Stone arrowheads were found in large numbers, while the number of bone and wood arrowheads decreased significantly. Stone arrowheads were sharper and able to bring a much greater harvest in hunting, and thus had taken the place of bone and wood arrowheads.

Handicrafts had been separated from agriculture, and non-agricultural laborers specialized in the production of pottery and jade had appeared. Pottery was still the main daily living utensils, and the pottery making technique was greatly improved compared to that in the Hemudu culture.

Pottery wheels were introduced into the production of a wide variety of pottery ware, including tripods, *dou*, pots, jars, ring-foot plates, ring-foot basins, *gui*, bowls, and cups, all regularly shaped. The black-coated clay pottery was particularly fine, representing the highest level of pottery making at the time. The piece of black-coated clay pottery finely engraved with the motif of a bird head and a snake body must have been made by a professional craftsman, for the clever and mysterious composition of the picture was achieved by smooth skillful lines, which was more than what an amateur could have done. Such time-consuming, finely carved pottery ware may have been transformed from a utilitarian vessel into a ceremonial vessel with a special purpose. String patterns, poked patterns, and openwork were common decorations on pottery. But most of the pottery wares were plain and unmarked, with the exception of cooking vessels, which were still decorated with some cord patterns.

In the Hemudu culture, the pottery *fu* was laid on three kettle supports during cooking. About 6,000 years ago, due to the influence of the Majiabang culture on the northern shore of Hangzhou Bay, a small number of tripods were made, but *fu* with supports still prevailed. By the time of the Liangzhu culture, which dated from around 5,300 years ago, the tripod had replaced the pottery *fu* as the main cooking vessel. As the body and legs of the tripod were often made separately and then glued together, the feet of the tripod were easily dislodged. So, a particularly large number of fin-shaped and T-shaped legs of tripods have been found all by themselves. Thus, it is difficult to tell whether the vessel is a tripod or a *fu* when only fragments of the body are found.

Vessels were divided into food containers and drink containers. The former include *dou*, plates, *gui*, *bo*, and bowls, which were less deep. Most of the vessels excavated were *dou*, which replaced bowls as the main serving vessels for individuals. They were very shallow and limited in capacity, with a long stem, which was easy for users sitting on the floor to pick up and eat directly. The function of the *bo* and bowl was similar to that of the *dou*, serving individual use, but they were found in much smaller numbers. So it can be inferred that gobbling from *bo* and other bowls was no longer common at the time. They were deeper, and thus more suitable for soupy meals or liquid food. The plate, basin, and *gui* were larger in size and seemed to have been food containers serving the whole group.

The presence of a large number of pottery drink containers indicated that wine drinking might have been common in the Liangzhu culture, although there was no solid physical evidence of alcohol. The excavated pottery containers for liquids include storage vessels such as double-nosed jugs (双鼻壶) and jars with tubular handles , drinking vessels such as cups, and heating vessels such as *he*. A number of filters were found in sites of the Liangzhu culture around the Taihu Lake. A type of filter, presumably used to separate wine and dregs (酒与糟), was found in the Wujiabu Site (吴家埠遗址), the Miaoqian Site, and the Fanshan Site in Yuhang District of Hangzhou City. Archeologists also found the elements of *Polygonum orientale*, commonly known as the yeast herb (酒曲草), from the Longnan Site in Wujiang County, Jiangsu Province, as a good evidence of alcohol making with the red polygonum (红蓼) as the yeast.

The production tools of the Liangzhu culture are mainly stone tools, with only a few wooden tools and bone tools excavated. Stone tools included stone plows, stone hoes, stone plowshares, stone scythes, and stone knives, stone adzes, stone axes, stone chisels, as well as stone spindle whorls, stone *yue*, carving tools, and stone arrowheads. Wooden tools included wooden oars, wooden adze handles, and wooden drills. The wooden drills were conical in shape, with a groove cut into the tip of the cone and a double-edged bone blade embedded in the groove, the other end being made into a small round tenon head for the attachment into a stem. Bone tools were rare, with only arrowheads, awls, and needles excavated.

In the Liangzhu culture around the Taihu Lake, jade craftsmanship was very well developed, forming jade pieces centered on ritual objects such as *cong*, *bi*, and *yue* as the core. Jade *cong* and *bi*, plus the comb-backed objects and jade cones, became the landmarks of the Liangzhu culture. In sharp contrast, there were few jade objects in the Ningbo area, most excavated items being decorative objects such as *jue*, *huang*, jade tubes, and jade cones, but no jade ritual objects have been found so far. This at least indicates that the influence of the Liangzhu culture on the south shore of Hangzhou Bay in terms of spiritual life might have been limited.

The building of earth platforms and altars was prevalent in various areas around the Taihu Lake in the Liangzhu culture. But there was only one rammed earth platform in the Ningbo area excavated in the Mingshanhou Site. It was surrounded by a deep ditch, which was also common around the earth platforms of the Liangzhu culture. Yet the remains of the burial and burning of sacrifices, which were indicative of ritual activities, have not been discovered so far.

In short, around 5,300 years ago, the Ningbo area started to be heavily influenced by the Liangzhu culture from around the Taihu Lake. However, the influence of the Liangzhu culture did not necessarily mean the complete loss of the local cultural tradition in the region. The ancients still retained and continued many of the regional traditions of the Hemudu culture, thus showing some characteristics that were very different from the typical Liangzhu culture. The traditions of the Hemudu culture inherent in the Ningbo area include the charcoal-tempered pottery, the cord pattern in pottery decoration, the pottery *fu* and *fu* supports. During the Liangzhu culture, the social organization around the Taihu Lake underwent a substantial change. The differences in the number of burial objects indicated the growing differentiation of social classes; the construction of large artificially stacked high-top graves and ceremonial facilities reflected the emergence of power. Jade ritual objects such as *cong*, *bi*, and jade *yue* were differentiated from utilitarian objects. But unlike the Liangzhu culture around the Taihu Lake, very few jade objects and no jade ritual objects have been found in Ningbo. Neither have we found large, high-profile burials with abundant funerary objects so far, which seems to indicate that the social differentiation of the Liangzhu culture in Ningbo was not yet significant.

XV. The Ancestors of the Baiyue People

During the Xia, Shang, and Zhou Dynasties, Zhejiang was the living area of the Yue people. In the late Spring and Autumn Period, Goujian, the King of Yue, built a powerful state, with the capital located in today's Shaoxing, and competed with the State of Wu. In 473 BC, the Yue forces conquered the State of Wu and marched north through the vast land of other states. Therefore, Goujian ranked among the Five Hegemons during the Spring and Autumn Period (春秋五霸). According to current research, it can be concluded that the supremacy of the Yue culture had its origins in the prehistoric cultures of Ningbo, with the Hemudu culture as one of the important sources.

The Yue people had many distinctive features. They worshiped the bird totem, cultivated rice, made stepped stone adzes, geometric stamped hard pottery, and primitive celadon, and were alleged to have lived on trees. Their skills of boat making, sailing, and sword-casting, their preference for peculiar foods, their habit of hair cutting and tattoo wearing, and their language were all different from those on the central plains. Almost all of these, with the exception of the hair-cutting, sword-casting, proto-celadon, and language, could be traced back to the prehistoric culture in Ningbo.

1. Bird Totem

As mentioned above, around 7,000 years ago, the Hemudu ancients already started to worship birds. About 60 bird-themed artifacts were found in the Hemudu culture. Most were not everyday utensils, which fully illustrated their bird-loving customs and bird totem worship. The bird totem still prevailed among the Yue people during the Liangzhu culture Period, as well as the Xia, Shang, and Zhou Dynasties, which very likely came from the Hemudu ancients. The Liangzhu culture black pottery pots with detailed bird carvings found at the Mingshanhou Site showed that the ancients in Ningbo still worshiped birds, and there were even more such instances of bird totems of the Liangzhu ancients around the Taihu Lake.

There are many records of the Yue bird-worship, one of which was the myth that during Yu's ruling, hundreds of birds kept tilling the low-lying field, and that after Yu's death, all the birds went away. When Wuyu (无 余), a prince of the Xia Dynasty, was enfeoffed the land whereupon he later founded the Yue Kingdom, he built a temple and worshiped Yu. Then, birds came back to the fields. But after the ruling of more than ten successors, Yu was no longer worshiped. Later, a newborn baby said that people should restore the previous rituals of sacrifice to Yu. This miracle was well received by the people and Yu-worship was recovered. Obviously, the "birds tilling field" must have been regarded as a symbol of good fortune. In the classic book the *Spring and Autumn Annals of Wu and Yue,* there is a record of "birds weeding the field in spring and cleaning the field pests in autumn", "with the alternation of seasons, coming and leaving regularly". Probably migratory birds such as geese were helping farmers get rid of pests and weeds. This is why, during the Han Dynasty, the magistrate of Shangyu District specifically ordered that "people were forbidden from harming the birds, and if they did, there would be no pardon for the punishment". An earlier reference to the bird-worship of the Yue people can be found in *Book of Documents* (《 尚 书 》): *"niao yi hui fu"* (鸟夷卉服， the bird-worshiping savages wove plants into suits). The term *"niao yi"* (鸟夷) was used to refer to a tribe of the Yue people with birds as their totem. In classic books of the Han Dynasty, such as the chapter "Yueshijia " (" 越世家 ", "The story of the Kings of the Yue Kingdom") of *Shi Ji*, it is recorded that the Yue people spoke a bird's language, and that King Goujian, its king, had the appearance of a bird with "a long-neck and a bird beak". Physical evidence of the Yue people's bird-worship was found in large numbers. For example, a bronze model of temple building was excavated in a late Spring and Autumn Period tomb in Potang Village (坡塘村), Shaoxing City. The temple was located on a square plane, with a pavilion roof topped with an octagonal spire and a big-tailed dove standing on it; inside the temple, six people were holding a ritual ceremony. In addition, a bronze *yue* from the Warring States Period was found in Yinzhou District. On the front side of the ax are four Yue people wearing feather crowns. Furthermore, a bronze cane was excavated with a large tailed turtledove (大尾鸠) standing on the top, with wings slightly were spread.

These objects are a good illustration of the Yue people's worship of the bird totem. What is more, during the late Spring and Autumn Period and the Warring States Period, the writing forms of characters in Yue was officially changed to the "bird seal" (鸟篆). The so-called bird seal was a conscious effort to change some strokes of each character into the shape of a bird (or add such strokes to a character), which served the purposes of both a esthetics and the bird totem worship. And such bird seal characters were engraved on weapons such as swords, *ge* (戈 , dagger-ax), and spears. In the case of the sword of King Goujian, excavated in Jiangling County, Hubei Province, eight bird seal characters — *yue wang jiu qian, zi zuo yong jian* (越王鸠浅，自作用剑) — were inscribed in two rows on the blade of the sword near the hilt, which means: "The sword has been made by and belongs to Jiuqian, King of the Yue." Such inscriptions on weapons were common.

The birds worshiped by the Hemudu people were mostly with hooked beaks and large tails, and were basically the same as the bird motifs on the jade *yue* and jade *bi* of the Liangzhu culture and the turtledoves on the bronze ware mentioned above. It seems that the turtledove has since evolved into the bird named Ye (冶鸟) referred to in *Soushenji* (《搜神记》) and the bird named Luoping (罗平鸟) in the *Wu-Yue Beishi* (《 吴越备史 》, *Complete History of Wu and Yue*).

The bird totem worship of the Yue people was also reflected in relics of the Han and Jin Dynasties, as well as in later documents and legends. Most Han Dynasty celadon ware from Shaoxing, Shangyu, Yuyao, and Cixi were decorated with bird motifs. Some of the more famous ones, such as funeral objects named *hunping* (魂瓶，soul jars), which were celadon jars with figures and pavilions and common in Yuyao and Cixi during the Western Jin Dynasty, were often decorated with many birds, human figures, and pavilions. And there were also celadon cups in the shape of birds from the Western Jin Dynasty excavated in Shangyu. These were clearly related to the long-standing local legend of birds as totems and deities, proving the profound influence of the bird totem worship from the Hemudu culture and the Yue culture.

2. Boat Making and Sailing

About 20 wooden oars and 3 ceramic boat models were found in the Hemudu culture, indicating that the Hemudu ancients were good at sailing. Their migration to the Zhoushan Islands about 6,000 years ago was the most convincing evidence of their ability to sail. Concerning the Liangzhu culture, besides wooden oars, there was a canoe hewn from a whole section of giant wood, with a pointed head and a square tail, were found well preserved in the ancient river at Maoshan Village (茅山村) in Linping Town (临平镇), Yuhang District. And a bamboo raft made of five interweaving bamboo strips was found at the Nanhu Lake in Yuhang District, still well preserved.

During the Spring and Autumn Period and the Warring States Period, the Yue people were renowned for their sailing skills. The book *Huainanzi* says: "The Hu (胡) people are good at horse-riding, but the Yue people are good at boat-making and sailing." In the chapter "Yanzhu Zhuan*"* (" 严助传 ", "The Story of Yan Zhu*")* *in Hanshu* (《汉书》 , *Book of Han*), it is said that "the Yue people are skilled in water fighting and can sail boats freely". King Goujian claimed that his people were "using boats as chariots and oars as horses, and could travel fast like riding on the wind". The Kingdom of Yue set up special government branches to manage shipbuilding and train naval divisions on a large scale. Their warships were named Yuhuangdazhou (余皇大舟， large boat), Louchuan (楼船， house boat), Gechuan (戈船， spear boat), Dayi (大翼， big-winged boat), Zhongyi (中翼， middle-winged boat), Xiaoyitumao (小翼突冒， small-winged boat), Xialaichuan (下濑船， flat-bottomed fast boats in shallow water) and so on, according to their functions and size; the other names — rafts, boats, canoes, plank boats, and yachts — were coined according to the form and structure of the water vehicles. A canoe from the Eastern Zhou Dynasty or later was excavated in Xizhu Town (西渚镇), Yixing County, Jiangsu Province; four canoes from the Spring and Autumn Period were excavated in the Yancheng Site (奄城 遗址), Wujin District, Changzhou City, Jiangsu Province; a canoe from the Warring States Period was excavated in Yuanping Town (苑坪镇), Wujiang District, Suzhou City, Jiangsu Province; and a canoe from the Warring States Period was also excavated in Shengzhou County, Zhejiang Province, loaded with a stamped hard pottery jar containing water chestnuts (菱角).

3. Rice Cultivation

As mentioned above, the Hemudu people lived on rice, and their rice farming was developed to the stage where plows were used as the production tools. The Yue people were also known for their expertise in rice cultivation, as recorded in the *Spring and Autumn Annals of Wu and Yue*: "The land of Yue was fertile and its yield was very good." More such records can be found in the chapter "Hequshu" (" 河渠书 ", "A Study of Rivers") of *Shi Ji* and the chapter "Gou Xu Zhi" (" 沟洫志 ", " Records of Rivers and Ditches") in *Hanshu*. For example, "The wasteland on the east bank of the river was given to the Yue people. They not only harvested enough rice to feed themselves but also paid tax with the surplus." This proves that up to the Western Han Dynasty, the Yue people were still the most skilled in rice cultivation. In the chapter "Huozhiliezhuan" (" 货殖列传 ", "Biographies of Merchants") of *Shi Ji*, "The land of Chu and Yue was vast and sparsely populated; people there lived on rice and fish." If we trace the origin of this "rice as the staple food, and fish as the main dish" (饭稻羹鱼) food custom, the Hemudu culture should have been an important source.

4. The Stilt House

The Hemudu stilt house was developed from the primitive nest house and adaptable to the hot and humid natural environment of the south, protecting people from heat, humidity, and animal attacks. At the Longnan

Site in Wujiang District, Suzhou City, Jiangsu Province, apart from semi-crypt houses and shallow-buried houses, stilt houses on the foundation of wood piles were also excavated. One such houses, 10 meters wide from east to west, was divided into three rooms, each 2.4–3.3 meters wide and 3.9 meters long. The three rooms were arranged side by side along a corridor of approximately 10 meters long and 1 meter wide on the south side of the house. The structure and form of this house were almost identical to those of the Hemudu culture. Most of the materials used in construction were organic, such as wood, bamboo, and thatch, which were not easily preserved. Therefore, complete stilt houses were rarely excavated. Fortunately, a plate with a ring-footed and a lid was found in the Xiantansi Site in Haiyan County, Zhejiang Province, on whose inner bottom was carved a stilt house, the lower part being wood piles (pillars), a floor upon the piles, and then some thicker pillars on the floor to support the upper part of the four sloping roofs. This is the earliest image of a stilt house ever seen.

The stilt house was still very popular among the Baiyue people (百越族). For example, the remains of a wood structure from the Spring and Autumn Period or maybe the Warring States Period were found at the Sanhetan Site (三合潭遗址), Yuhuan County, with a complete layout made up of more than 100 densely arranged piles and pillars large or small. Its construction might have consisted the following steps: digging out a hole in the earth, matting the hole with boards, driving piles into the matted holes, laying the floor upon the piles, and setting up the living space on the floor. Furthermore, the stilt house was also found in Gouzhang of Ningbo. Today, the stilt house, once prevalent among the Yue people, remains popular among many people in the southwest of China.

5. Stepped Stone Adzes

The stepped stone adze refers to a special type of stone adzes with a stepped ridge on the upper back, which makes a composite tool with a wooden or bone handle. The function of the stepped ridge was to facilitate its tying or fitting to the handle, thus extending the arm reach. Stepped stone adzes have been found in many places in Southeast China and in the South Pacific islands. Archeologists believe that the arc-backed stone adzes found in the Hemudu culture was the original form of stepped stone adzes. From the arc-backed stone adze to the stepped stone adze the form evolution of adzes in the Hemudu culture was coherent. When the Liangzhu Culture stage reached its golden times, the Hemudu stone adzes gradually spread to the surrounding areas. Three paths of transmission were identified:

The northern route can be further divided into two: the first spread to Shandong Province via northern Jiangsu Province, and then across Bohai Bay (渤海湾) to the Liaodong Peninsula, with a sub-branch spreading across the Yellow Sea from the Shandong Peninsula to the Korean Peninsula, and then spreading southward across the Tsushima Strait (对马海峡) to Japan; the second went from northern Jiangsu Province through Anhui Province to Henan Province.

The western route started from Zhejiang Province and went to Jiangxi Province and southern Anhui Province; one branch continued westwards into Hubei Province and Hunan Province while the other turned southwards into Guangdong Province, where it merged with the indigenous culture of the Pearl River Delta, resulting in another distinctive form, the shouldered and stepped stone adze, and then furthered its spreading southwest to Guangxi Autonomous Region, Guizhou Province, and Yunnan Province.

The southern route went from Zhejiang Province into Fujian Province, crossed the sea to Taiwan Province of China, and finally arrived in the Philippines. From the Philippines, the stone adzes were spread to Indonesia in the west, Polynesia in the east, and New Zealand in the south.

From the above, it can be seen that the stepped stone adzes created by the Hemudu ancients were spread far and wide, and their influence was so profound that they had written a glorious page in the history of ancient culture in China and abroad.

During the Shang and Zhou Dynasties, the Yue people began to make bronze production tools, but traditional stone production tools continued to be in use. In archeological excavations of village sites of these periods in Ningbo, numerous stepped stone adzes were found, with more elaborate processing than before, but significantly fewer than during the heyday of the Liangzhu culture.

6. *Fu, Fu* Supports, and Duck-shaped Pots

The pottery *fu* and the matching supports, with their well-developed cord patterns and distinctive shapes, were the most characteristic cooking vessels in use throughout the Hemudu culture. It is interesting to note that all the cooking vessels of the Liangzhu culture were pottery tripods, and only a few pottery *fu* survived in the Ningbo area. But no matching supports for them were excavated. During the Xia, Shang, and Zhou Dynasties, sandy clay pottery *fu* and supports reappeared in the region, still decorated with cord patterns by stamping. The pottery *he* of the Hemudu culture was different from the pottery *he* of the Majiabang culture. The former was shaped like a leather bag, with a handle placed between the mouth of the vessel and the tubular spout in one line, while the handle of the latter was placed on the side of the abdomen, with the spout and handle forming a right angle. A large number of duck-shaped pots were excavated from other sites of the Shang Dyansty and the Zhou Dynasty in Shangyu District, Cixi County, and Yingzhou District, and their shape is quite close to the pottery *he* of the Hemudu culture.

7. Stamped Hard Pottery with Geometric Patterns

The remains of stamped hard pottery from the Xia, Shang, and Zhou Dynasties have been excavated throughout the whole province. The geometric patterns stamped on pottery ware have also been found in artifacts of the Hemudu culture, for example, the diagonal lines and woven patterns carved on the bone dagger handle, and the geometric decorative motifs on the wooden oars, the wood carved fish-shaped handle, the carved cup-shaped ivory vessel, the serrated bone vessel, the wood panel components, and the pottery spindle whorl, the carved pottery block, and the pottery *yu*. Moreover, the pottery spindle whorls and the carved potsherds were also decorated with the wave pattern and a pattern roughly resembling the cloud and thunder pattern. The woven pattern of reed mats could have been the origin of woven patterns (otherwise known as straw mat patterns) on stamped pottery.

8. Domestication of Dogs

Dogs were cherished as faithful companions of human beings. Most of the dog skulls found in the Hemudu culture were relatively intact, with some exceptions broken smoothly along the bone seams, instead of being intentionally cracked open, whereas the skulls of other animals were cracked on purpose, indicating that the ancients treated dogs differently from the way they did other animals. The large amount of dog dung found around the houses, containing a large number of finely crushed animal bones such as fish bones, was another reflection of the closeness between dogs and the Hemudu people. Similarly, dogs occupied an important place in the minds of the Yue people, as recorded in the chapter *"Goujian Fa Wu Waizhuan"* (" 勾践伐吴外传 ", "Goujian's Campaign Against Wu") of *Wu-Yue Chunqiu*, Goujian's incentives for reproduction were "a jug of wine and a dog, when two boys were born; a jug of wine and a pig, when two girls were born". Since boys were more valued at that time, it can be concluded that dogs must have been regarded as a more valuable reward than pigs. This dog-valuing custom has been preserved among the descendants of the Yue people living in today's Taizhou, Wenzhou, Lishui (丽水), and the border areas between Zhejiang Province and Fujian Province, where "dogs are sacrificed when parents die". The dog offering to the parents and ancestors is surely good evidence of the importance of the dog in the hearts of the Yue people.

9. Monkey Brain Eating

After the identification of monkey skulls excavated from the Hemudu culture by paleontologists, it was concluded that the Hemudu people had a monkey-brain-eating custom. As recorded in *Linhai Shuitu Yiwuzhi* (《 临海水土异物志 》, *Records of Peculiar Things along the Coast*) by Shen Ying (沈莹), a scholar in the Three Kingdoms Period, it was also thought that the Yue descendants "all favored monkey brain soup, which was served with vegetables to wake the drunken up. A popular saying is that Yue people would rather owe others a huge sum of money than enjoy their treat of monkey brain soup without giving a return banquet. The use of monkey brains as a delicacy was also recorded by Li Shizhen (李时珍) in his *Compendium of Materia Medica* (《本草纲目》) and is still practiced in Guangdong, Fujian and Zhejiang Provinces. To sum up, there is a close kinship between the Hemudu culture and the Yue culture, the former being an important source of the latter. This has been affirmed and supported by more and more experts and scholars.

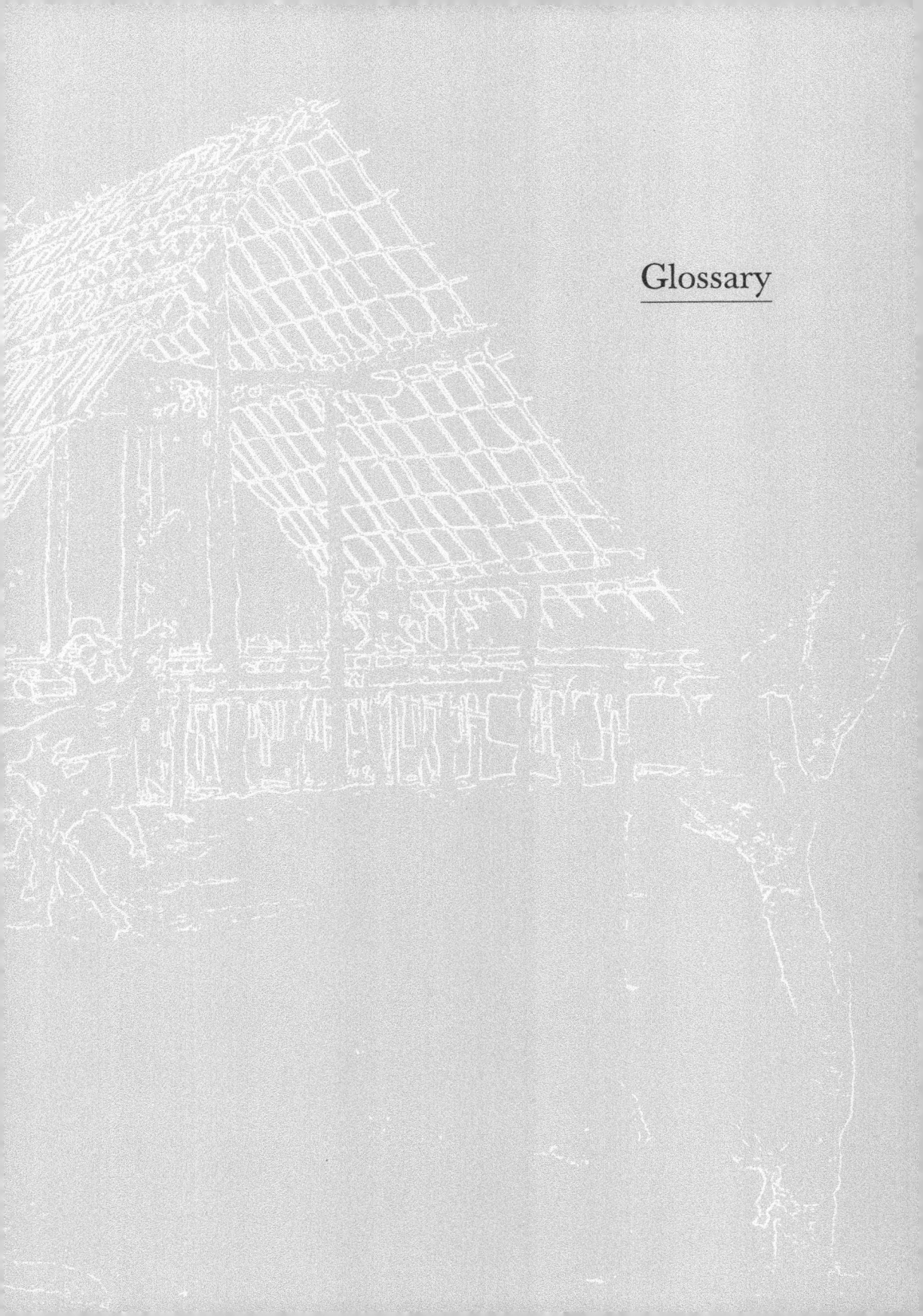

Glossary

Chinese	English
阿波罗	Apollo
阿狄多	Aditya
安志敏	An Zhimin
暗红色叶蜡石	dark red pyrophyllite
八字桥村	Baziqiao Village
百越文化	the Baiyue culture
百越族	the Baiyue people
板瓦	tile
半坡遗址	the Banpo Site
薄叶桨	thin-bladed oar
保国寺	the Baoguo Temple
北龙岛	the Beilong Island
《本草纲目》	*Compendium of Materia Medica*
彼德·贝尔伍德	Peter Bellwood
璧	*bi* (disk)
卞家山遗址	the Bianjiashan Site
鳖类	soft-shelled turtle
波利尼西亚人	Polynesian
钵	*bo* (bowl)
伯益	Bo Yi
渤海湾	Bohai Bay
沧源佤族自治县	Cangyuan Va Autonomous County
藏书文化系列	ancient libraries
曹娥江	the Cao'e River
草鞋山遗址	the Caoxieshan Site

茶多酚	polyphenols
豺	jackal
柴桥镇	Chaiqiao Town
陈文华	Chen Wenhua
城山渡	the Chengshan Ferry
丞相	*chengxiang* (prime minister)
赤皮稠	red-bark oak (*Quercus gilva*)
冲天嘴	upward mouth
锄耕	hoe-tillage
储备粮	food reserve
楚国	the Vassal Kingdom of Chu
穿山甲	pangolin
船宫	boat palace
窗格纹	latticework
槌	mallet
春秋五霸	the Five Hegemons during the Spring and Autumn Period
慈城镇	Cicheng Town
慈湖遗址	the Cihu Site
慈南山地	the Cinan Hills
磁山	the Cishan Mountain
磁山遗址	the Cishan Site
琮	*cong* (jade)
崔广	Cui Guang
打桩立柱	stilt half driven into the ground
大埠头村	Dabutou Village
大尾鸠	large tailed turtledove

大汶口	Dawenkou
大翼	*Dayi* (big-winged boats)
大竹山岛	Dazhushan Island
带卯眼榫	tenon with mortises
丹城镇	Dancheng Town
丹尼尔·威尔逊	Daniel Wilson
刀耕火种	slash-and-burn
稻作农业印度起源说	the Indian origin of rice farming
稻作文化	rice culture
地层	strata
点种棒	seed dibble
丁村	Dingcun
鼎	tripod
定经杆	the warp beam
东安乡	Dong'an Town
豆	*dou* (stemmed bowl)
渡头村	Dutou Village
渡头山	the Dutou Mountain (the Ferry Mountain)
断木为杵，掘地为臼	cutting wood into pestles and digging the ground into a mortar to process rice
对马海峡	the Tsushima Strait
二六市镇	Erliushi Town
法家	the Legalist School
反山遗址	the Fanshan Site
饭稻羹鱼	rice as the staple food and fish as the main dish
方格纹	trellis pattern

非洲稻	African rice (*Oryza glaberrima*)
酚酶同功酶电泳法	phenolase isozyme electrophoresis
奉化江	the Fenghua River
福泉	Fuquan (Happiness Spring)
福泉桥	the Fuquan Bridge
福泉山遗址	the Fuquanshan Site
釜	*fu*（cauldron）
釜底抽薪	*fu di chou xin* (removing the burning wood under the boiling pot so as to solve the problem once and for all)
覆船	Fuchuan (Overturned Boat)
复合型农业生产工具	composite agricultural production tool
复活节岛	Easter Island
傅家山遗址	the Fujiashan Site
高塘岛	the Gaotang Island
戈	*ge* (dagger-axe)
戈船	*gechuan* (spear-equipped boat)
耕作技术	farming technique
工字形的	I-shaped
勾践	Goujian
《勾践伐吴外传》	*Goujian Fa Wu Waizhuan* (*Goujian's Campaign against Wu*)
钩栲	Castanopsis tibetana
句余山	the Gouyu Mountains
句章城	Gouzhang City
古建筑与纪念建筑系列	ancient and memorial architectures
骨匕	bone dagger

骨笄	bone hairpin
骨哨	bone whistle
骨匙	bone spoon
骨耜	bone *si*
骨耜方銎	the square hole of a plowshare
骨鱼镖	bone fish dart
骨针	bone needle
骨锥	bone awl
刮削器	scraper
龟形陶盉	the turtle-shaped pottery *he*
硅藻	diatom
鬹	*gui* (tripod with three hollow legs)
簋	*gui* (food container with two handles)
锅	*guo* (pot)
锅巴	potpourri stuck to the inner bottom
国家级历史文化名城	a historical and cultural city at the national level
海门	Haimen
海防史迹系列	historic sites of sea defense
海外交通史系列	historic sites of overseas transportation
《韩非子》	*Hanfeizi*
《韩非子·五蠹》	"Five Bookworms" of the book *Han Feizi*
《汉书》	*Hanshu* (*Book of Han*)
《汉书·沟洫志》	"Gou Xu Zhi" ("Records of Rivers and Ditches") in *Hanshu*
《汉书·严助传》	"Yanzhu Zhuan" ("The Story of Yan Zhu") in *Hanshu*

貉	raccoon dog
盉	*he* (pitch)
河姆渡村	Hemudu Village
河姆渡文化	the Hemudu culture
《河姆渡文化初探》	*A Preliminary Exploration of the Hemudu Culture*
河姆渡先民	the Hemudu people
《河姆渡——新石器时代遗址考古发掘报告》	*Hemudu—Archeology and Excavation Report of Sites in the Neolithic Age*
河姆渡遗址	the Hemudu Site
河姆渡遗址第1次考古发掘座谈会	Symposium on the First Phase of Hemudu Archeological Excavation
《河姆渡遗址第一期发掘报告》	*Excavations (First Seacon) at Ho-Mu-Tu in Yu-Yao County, Chekiang Province*
黑色陶衣	black pottery coating
黑熊	black bear
横河镇	Henghe Town
横溪镇	Hengxi Town
红蓼	red polygonum
红烧土祭台	sintered clay altar
厚粥烂饭	thick porridge
淮河流域	the Huaihe River Region
《淮南子》	*Huainanzi*
《淮南子·天文篇》	"The Chapter on Astronomy" of *Huainanzi*
槐树籽	acacia seed
璜	*huang* (pendant)
黄帝	Yellow Emperor

黄公	Huang Gong
黄墓渡	Huangmudu
黄婆山	the Huangpo Hill
黄宗羲	Huang Zongxi
回纹	rectangular spiral pattern
汇观山遗址	the Huiguanshan Site
汇头村	Huitou Village
火焰纹	fire pattern
吉野里遗址	the Yoshinogari Site
假灵芝	*Ganoderma atrum*
尖状器	pointed tool
江浙钓樟	camphor tree
绞纱棒	hank bar
介形虫	ostracods
金关恕	Kansuke Kim
金塘镇	Jintang Town
近代史迹系列	other important sites in relation with modern history
粳稻	japonica rice
井口	the mouth of the well
酒曲草	the yeast herb
酒与糟	wine and dreg
玦	*jue* (jade)
康熙	Kangxi
《考古学报》	*Journal of Archeology*
壳丘头	Keqiutou
刻花木构件	carved wood component

刻划戳印	incising and stamping
孔虫	foraminifera
跨湖桥文化	the Kuahuqiao culture
跨湖桥遗址	the Kuahuqiao Site
老虎山遗址	the Laohushan Site
耒	*lei* (a farming tool for dibbling and digging holes)
李培基	Li Peiji
李时珍	Li Shizhen
利仓	Li Cang
立鸟形状	standing-bird form
砺石	grindstone
鬲形的	*li*-shaped
连体双鸟	conjoined birds
良渚文化	the Liangzhu culture
良渚文化名山后类型	the Mingshanhou type of the Liangzhu culture
梁	beam
梁头榫	tenon at the end of the beam
蓼	polygonum
《临海水土异物志》	*Linhai Shuitu Yiwuzhi (Records of Peculiar Things along the Coast)*
林惠祥	Lin Huixiang
临平镇	Linping Town
菱角	water chestnut
菱形纹	rhombus pattern
刘邦	Liu Bang
刘盈	Liu Ying

刘泽纯	Liu Zechun
龙南遗址	the Longnan Site
龙山文化	the Longshan culture
楼船	*Louchuan* (house-boat)
芦山寺村	Lushansi Village
《芦山寺志》	*Chronicles of Lushan Temple*
罗伯特·海尼-格尔顿	Robert Heine-Geldern
罗春华	Luo Chunhua
罗家角遗址	the Luojiajiao Site
罗江	Luojiang
罗江公社	Luojiang Commune
罗平鸟	the bird named Luoping
吕后	Empress Lü
麻布纹	linen pattern
马家浜文化	the Majiabang culture
马来人	Malay
马桥文化	the Maqiao culture
马桥镇	Maqiao Town
马王堆汉墓遗址	the Mawangdui Han Tomb Site
慢轮修整技术	the slow-wheel trimming technique
毛家嘴	Maojiazui
茅冈	Maogang
茅山村	Maoshan Village
茅山遗址	the Maoshan Site
美拉尼西亚人	Melanesian
美玉	beautiful jade
弥生文化	the Yayoi culture

密克罗尼西亚人	Micronesian
苗族	the Miao nationality
庙岛群岛	the Miaodao Islands
名山后村	Mingshanhou Village
名山后遗址	the Mingshanhou Site
明伟村	Mingwei Village
亩	*mu*
木构水井	wooden well
木臼	wooden mortar
木磨棒	rod
木耜	wooden *si*
南岛语族文化	the Austronesian culture
南湖	the Nanhu Lake
南浦乡	Nanpu Town
南亚野生沼泽水牛	wild swamp buffalo in South Asia
泥质陶	clay pottery
鸟形器（蝶形器）	bird-shaped vessel
《鸟夷》	*niao yi*
鸟夷卉服	*niao yi hui fu*（the bird-worshiping savages wove plants into suits）
鸟越宪三郎	Kenzaburo Torigoe
鸟篆	bird seal
宁波古物陈列所	Ningbo Museum of Antiquities
宁绍平原	the Ningbo-Shaoxing Plain
藕	lotus root
配套水利灌溉设施	supporting irrigation facilitiy
彭东乡	Pengdong Town

平身柱卯眼	middle column mortise
平潭岛	the Pingtan Island
坡塘村	Potang Village
破釜沉舟	*po fu chen zhou* (breaking the pot and destroying the ship so as to perish the hope of a retreat)
破土器	soil breaker
漆碗	acquered bowl
企口板	rabbet joint
前溪湖遗址	the Qianxihu Site
钱岙遗址	the Qian'ao Site
钱山漾遗址	the Qianshanyang Site
乾隆	Qianlong
芡实	Gorgon fruit
桥头镇	Qiaotou Town
青墩遗址	the Qingdun Site
青铜錞	the bronze *chun*
人工夯筑土台	rammed square platform
三合潭遗址	the Sanhetan Site
三江口	Sanjiangkou
三江平原	the Sanjiang Plain
三七市镇	Sanqishi Town
沙马士	Shamashi
沙溪遗址	the Shaxi Site
山茶属	genus Camellia
《山海经》	*Shanhaijing (The Classics of Mountains and Rivers)*

山鸡椒	Litsea cubeba
商山	the Shangshan Mountain
上山遗址	the Shangshan Site
《尚书》	*Book of Documents*
沈莹	Shen Ying
十过	Shiguo
十字斗口	cross mortise
石锛	stone adze
石刀	stone knife
石斧	stone axe
石镰	stone scythe
石磨盘	stone grinding ball
石耨	stone hoe
石球	stone ball
石丸	stone pellet
石寨山遗址	the Shizhaishan Site
石珠	stone bead
石镞	stone arrowhead
《史记》	*Shi Ji (The Records of the Grand Historian)*
《史记·河渠书》	"Hequshu" ("A Study of Rivers") in *Shiji*
《史记·货殖列传》	"Huozhiliezhuan" ("Biographies of Merchants") in *Shiji*
《史记·留侯世家》	"The Story of Marquis Liu" in *Shiji*
《史记·越世家》	"The Story of the Kings of the Yue Kingdom" in *Shiji*
史前文化系列	prehistoric cultural sites
氏族墓地	clan cemetery

《世本》	*Shiben*
双鼻壶	double-nosed jug
双耳平底罐	flat-footed jar with two ears
双飞燕	double swallows
双鸟朝阳	the birds with the sun
水田畈遗址	the Shuitianfan Site
舜	Shun
《说苑》	*Shuoyuan*
四明山	the Siming Mountains
《四明山志》	*A Record of the Siming Mountains*
耜	*si* (plow)
耜耕	si-tillage
耜耕农业阶段	the *si*-tillage stage
崧泽文化	the Songze culture
《搜神记》	*Soushenji (Stories of Immortals)*
苏秉琦	Su Bingqi
《苏格兰考古与史前学年鉴》	*The Archaeology and Prehistoric Annals of Scotland*
酸枣	jujube
榫	tenon
榫卯技术	tenon-and-mortise work
榫头	tenon joint
塔山遗址	the Tashan Site
台西遗址	the Taixi Site
苔	moss
汤谷	the Tang Valley
汤山	the Tangshan Mountain

汤圣祥	Tang Shengxiang
陶纺轮	pottery spindle whorl
陶罐	ceramic cauldron
陶臼	pottery mortar
陶拍	pottery paddle
陶寺遗址	the Taosi Site
天台山	the Tiantai Mountains
田螺山遗址	the Tianluoshan Site
樋口隆康	Takayasu Higuchi
童岙村	Tong'ao Village
童家岙遗址	the Tongjia'ao Site
筒	cylinder
筒瓦	imbrex
团结村	Tuanjie Village
瓦当	eave tile
汪济英	Wang Jiying
王家坝村	Wangjiaba Village
王士伦	Wang Shilun
圩墩遗址	the Weidun Site
文化层	cultural layer
瓮棺葬	urn burial
《倭族之源——云南》	*Yunnan—The Origin of the Japanese*
无余	Wuyu
吴家埠遗址	the Wujiabu Site
吴王	the King of Wu
《吴越备史》	*Wu-Yue Beishi (Complete History of Wu and Yue)*

《吴越春秋》	*Wu-Yue Chunqiu (Annals of Wu and Yue)*
《吴越春秋·勾践伐吴外传》	"Goujian Fa Wu Waizhuan" ("Goujian's Campaign Against Wu") in *Wu-Yue Chunqiu*
西盟佤族自治县	Ximeng Va Autonomous County
西渚镇	Xizhu Town
下濑船	Xiatachuan (flat-bottomed fast boat in shallow waters)
仙人洞遗址	the Xianrendong Cave Site and the Diaotonghuan Cave Site
仙坛庙遗址	the Xiantanmiao Site
籼稻	indica rice
籼亚种中晚稻型水稻	Oryza Sativa L. subsp hsien Ting
锹	shovel
相岙村	Xiang'ao Village
鲞架山遗址	the Xiangjiashan Site
象山半岛	Xiangshan Peninsula
橡子	acorn
销钉	pin
小东门	the Xiaodongmen Gate
小东门遗址	the Xiaodongmen Site
《小尔雅·广物》	"Guangwu" of the ancient dictionary *Xiao'erya*
小黄山遗址	the Xiaohuangshan Site
小南海	Xiaonanhai
小翼突冒	*Xiaoyitumao* (small-winged boat)
斜纹或人字纹	twill or herringbone pattern
许金耀	Xu Jinyao

熏烤	smoke
亚热带季风气候区	the subtropical monsoon climate zone
亚微结构	sub-micro structure
亚洲稻	Asian rice (*Oryza sativa*)
亚洲象	Asian elephant
严文明	Yan Wenming
奄城遗址	the Yancheng Site
燕尾榫	dovetail joint
杨鸿勋	Yang Hongxun
杨歧岙遗址	the Yangqi'ao Site
仰韶	Yangshao
仰韶文化	the Yangshao culture
姚江	the Yuyao River
姚江谷地	the Yuyao River Valley
瑶山	Yaoshan
冶鸟	the bird named Ye
薏仁	grain of Job's tears
鄞奉平原	Yinzhou-Fenghua Plain
印度阿萨姆—中国云南地区起源说	the Assam-Yunnan origin of rice farming
印纹陶文化	the Stamped Pottery culture
印纹硬陶	stamped hard pottery
颖	*ying* (the ear of the grain)
甬	Yong (Ningbo)
甬江	the Yongjiang River
有巢	Youchao (Nest Owner)
有段石锛	stepped stone adze

余慈平原	the Yuyao-Cicheng Plain
盂	*yu* (jar)
余皇大舟	*Yuhuangdazhou* (large boat)
俞为洁	Yu Weijie
鱼藻纹盆	fish-and-algae basin
禹	Yu
玉蟾岩洞穴遗址	the Yuchanyan Cave Site
元宝山	the Yuanbao Mountain
原始纺织技术	primitive textile skill
原始农业	primitive agriculture
原始织机	primitive loom
苑坪镇	Yuanping Town
钺	*yue* (battle-axe)
《越绝书》	*Glory of the Yue*
越人	the Yue people
越王	the King of Yue
越窑青瓷窑址系列	ruins of Yue celadon kiln
云南元谋人	Yuanmouensis
灶坑	hearth pit
甑	*zeng* (steamer)
馕粥	congee
张光直	Kwang-chih Chang
张陵山遗址	the Zhanglingshan Site
丈亭镇	Zhangting Town
招宝山	the Zhaobao Hill
浙东学派史迹系列	historic sites of Eastern Zhejiang School

《浙江河姆渡遗址第二次发掘的主要收获》	"The Second Excavation of the Hemudu Site in Zhejiang Province"
浙江农业大学	Zhejiang Agicultural University
浙江省博物馆	Zhejiang Provincial Museum
浙江省第一届亦工亦农考古培训班	The First Archeological Training Class for Half-farmer-half-workers
浙江文物管理委员会	the Administrative Committee of Cultural Relics of Zhejiang Province
浙江自然博物馆	Zhejiang Museum of Natural History
芝林溪	the Zhilin Creek
直棂栏杆卯眼	lattice railing mortise
直筒形水井	straight well
铚	*zhi* (sickle)
中国传统榫卯木构建筑技术	Chinese traditional tenon-and-mortise technique
中翼	*Zhongyi* (middle-winged boat)
中原地区	the central plains
舟室	boat hall
周口店	Zhoukoudian
周口店遗址	the Zhoukoudian Site
《周易》	*Zhouyi* (*Book of Changes*)
竹节把豆	*dou* (stemmed bowl) with bamboo-shaped handles
竹木筏	bamboo raft
柱	column
柱头柱脚榫	head tenon and foot tenon on the column
爪哇犀	the Javan rhinocero

转角柱卯眼	corner pillar mortise
鯔山遗址	the Zishan Site
综杆	heddle shaft
佐藤洋一郎	Yoichiro Sato

译后记

　　本书的原文本《东方曙光：宁波史前文明》系"宁波文化丛书"（第一辑）》之一册，是一本普及性的文化读物，介绍了宁波史前文明的两个阶段——河姆渡文化和良渚文化，揭示了宁波境内这两个文化之间的过渡，并从干栏式建筑、稻作农业、动物驯养、渔猎采集、挖井取水、编织纺织、舟楫制作、陶器制作、爱美之心、太阳崇拜等十余个方面详细描述了宁波史前文明的细节。本书集知识性、学术性与普及性于一体，为大众提供了一本迅速了解宁波史前文明的口袋书。

　　本书的翻译和出版工作得到了宁波大学科学技术学院人文学院的资助与支持，尤其要感谢人文学院的周志锋院长、贺安芳副院长和项霞副院长的指导和帮助。

　　虽然只是普及读物，但本书的专业性很突出。词汇层面，特别是一些考古学术语确实给译者带来了不小的挑战。例如，与干栏式建筑、陶器和石器相关的词语特别多，尤其是在细节方面，译者查阅了大量的相关资料和工具书，请教了考古学专业人士，翻译时力求做到忠实原文和事实，采用音译、直译以及加注的策略，为译文读者提供尽量多的相关信息，以帮助他们理解和接受。本书内容具有较强的专业性，相信英语读者中也有不少是专业研究人员，为方便他们查阅，书中的文化负载词第一次出现时，基本上有对应的中文表达置于该词语之后。

　　此外，为了让普通英语读者产生较好的阅读体验，译者也做了如下努力。一方面，考虑到本书的普及性，译文尽量选用贴近日常生活的词汇，避免过于学术和晦涩的表述，以使读者不太费力即可读懂本书。另一方面，本书原文中的某些考古细节，对于一般读者是较大考验，译者经斟酌后稍做删除，以减轻读者的认知负荷，实现本书作为口袋书的快乐阅读的目的。

　　最后，感谢原作者提供了许多第一手的考古图片，使译文在图片的辅助下更具可读性。

　　怀胎十月，翻译本书亦用了十月，幸得到董铁柱老师和黄静芬老师的指点，做了很多改进，在此诚表谢意！由于译者水平有限，译文一定还有许多不足之处，还请方家不吝赐教。